Georges Giacometti, Edgar Whitaker

Russia's work in Turkey: a revelation

Georges Giacometti, Edgar Whitaker

Russia's work in Turkey: a revelation

ISBN/EAN: 9783743316164

Manufactured in Europe, USA, Canada, Australia, Japa

Cover: Foto ©Suzi / pixelio.de

Manufactured and distributed by brebook publishing software (www.brebook.com)

Georges Giacometti, Edgar Whitaker

Russia's work in Turkey: a revelation

RUSSIA'S WORK IN TURKEY:

A REVELATION.

FROM THE FRENCH

"LES RESPONSABILITÉS"

OF

G. GIACOMETTI.

TRANSLATED BY

EDGAR WHITAKER.

"O præclarum custodem ovium (ut aiunt) lupum!"
Cic. Philip. iii. 11.

LONDON:
EFFINGHAM WILSON, ROYAL EXCHANGE, E.C.
1877.

PREFACE.

"LES RESPONSABILITÉS," of which the following pages are a translation, appeared in Constantinople only just before the diplomatic exodus which ensued upon the *fiasco* of the Conference. Had the work been published earlier, Mr. Gladstone's pious aspiration that England should "emulate the good deeds of Russia" might probably never have been uttered, or, if uttered, would have failed to arouse the enthusiasm which responded to it. Moreover, certain plenipotentiaries at the Conference might have cut better figures and served better ends, had the knowledge against which they fortified themselves been forced upon them by a timely disclosure of these secret workings of the policy which they supported with almost offensive ostentation.

To the delicacy or timidity of the Porte is due the long delay of this disclosure. The existence of the documents which compose it has been known to the Porte for the last two or three years, but the holders of the prize were unable to obtain permission to give them publicity. There was always the fear of envenoming the diplomatic relations between the Porte and St. Petersburg, and so the Turk hid the fox in his bosom and suffered his vitals to be gnawed away rather than commit a diplomatic *maladresse*.

The interest of the book as a piece of political scandal was to some extent forestalled in Constantinople by the fact that several of the mines of General Ignatieff—the Mr. X of these pages—had been sprung before the work appeared. Close bystanders had thus been able to recognise the engineer in the style of his work, and many a buried fact cast upon the surface by successive explosions had already taught them how dark and strange was the fashion of his burrowings.

But, just in proportion as its sensational colour faded, so its historical and dramatic interest grew more hotly vivid from this very cause; for men who had seen a part wanted to know the whole, and craved to unravel all the mysteries of the plot of which they had witnessed the bloody *denouement*.

The pages of "Les Responsabilités" did not, it is true, exhaust the subject; but they pieced together the fragments of knowledge already acquired; linked in a connected tale the scattered phenomena which had been the signs of their times in Constantinople, Jerusalem, Antioch, Mount Athos and other fields in which Russia labours; threw a distinct light upon the origin of the insurrection in Bosnia and Herzegovina; and exposed the complex dealings by which the unfortunate Bulgarians were involved in a revolt with which they had no real sympathy. They revealed, moreover, the real feebleness of the hold of the Panslavic idea upon the South-Slavic peoples, showing the idea to be kept alive in that ungenial soil only by the golden stream with which Russia assiduously waters it.

But, satisfactory as all this was to the student of current history, to the politician it yielded only regret that the disclosure should have come too late to exercise any influence upon the forces which were shaping events. Thus, the author's flattering proposal that I should undertake to prepare an English version of his work did not meet with immediate acquiescence, because I failed to see what practical good it could do at so late an hour, and when the popular interest in England on Eastern affairs seemed to be fast cooling down.

While thus hesitating, the telegraph brought the news that the indefatigable General had quitted his retreat at Krussodernitza and was starting on a series of missions to the principal Courts of Europe. The news was speedily followed by a whisper that the object of this movement was to induce the Powers to cast the tatters of the Treaty of Paris to the winds, and to suffer Russia to creep back into her old position as "protectress" of the Christian races subject to the Porte,—the position from which it was the object of the Crimean war to dislodge her, and of the Ninth article of the Treaty to shut her permanently out.

This move of Russian diplomacy creates a new opportunity and fitness for the publication of an English version of Mr. Giacometti's work, which reflects, as in a mirror, the nature of the "protectorate" which Russia aspires to exercise over the Christian peoples of Turkey, and the manner of her manipulation of it;—discovers Russia in fact hard at her holy work, bathed in a sweat of lies, her bared arms plunged now in blood and now in gold.

As regards the authenticity of the letters, no independent person, competent to form a judgment upon them, has ventured to dispute it. On the other hand, those competent to judge have accepted them without misgiving. And, indeed, the correspondence bears upon its face the stamp of truth. In the style and phraseology of Mr. X's letters, in the tone of their raillery and sarcasm, in the *naive* frankness of their cynicism, the language of General Ignatieff is unmistakable. Add to this the extraordinary knowledge of detail which the letters display,—of men, of things, of places, over all the vast scene in which the action lies, and the conviction is forced upon the reader's mind, that none but the hand which, with consummate skill was guiding that action, could have touched upon all these with the freedom and firmness of Mr. X., and escape as he has done every incongruity and inaccuracy.

EDGAR WHITAKER.

Pera, Constantinople; *March* 16, 1877.

CYPHERED KEY.

If the reader has been pleased to honour with any degree of his attention our preceding publications he will be aware that we have a delicacy with regard to the use of proper names.

We feel this delicacy even with respect to those collective beings which are called Powers—States. It will be understood that we respect the sentiment all the more when persons are in question.

We would not, however, inflict upon the reader the task which we ourselves have had to undertake, of guessing at the Cyphers of Departments, Embassies, Consulates, and Secret Societies. Not to associate him, therefore, with our labours beyond a reasonable degree, we have limited ourselves to composing for his use the following cyphered key:

Mr. X . . . is a high personage residing at Constantinople.

Mr. Y . . . is his colleague residing at Vienna.

Mr. Z . . . is the chief of the Asiatic department of a great European Power.

Monseigneur * is an august personage.

Monseigneur * *, a near relative of the preceding, is an august personage of the same rank.

Monseigneur * * *, a personage yet more august, is the heir apparent of a great empire.

Monseigneur * * * * is a personage who cannot be called august, but who reigns over a people of 120,000 souls.

Monseigneur * * * * *, another personage by no means august, governs a country over which he has more than once attempted to reign.

As regards the actors of minor importance whom this publication will introduce to the stage, their names will be simply represented by dotted lines. The part which they play is alone of value to our theme.

The reader will pardon us for imposing on him this slight trouble. It was indispensable to adopt some such method.

We treat of a subject which, in a certain point of view, is a lofty one; it presents however details which call for severe comment. But we shall be careful never to allow the *severities* of our pen to be confounded with *personalities*.

THE RESPONSIBILITIES.

I.

The hour is a solemn one. Out of the decisions taken at Constantinople there must come peace, or perhaps, war. Europe anxiously listens to the voice of the oracles which the telegraph transmits to her from hour to hour, and she asks herself from minute to minute whether she ought to be alarmed or to rejoice.

If peace is to result from the negotiations of which the *Tershané* palace* has been the theatre, let peace be welcome. None will rejoice at it more than Turkey will, for no power has greater need than Turkey for peace, tranquility and leisure. She has need of these things in order to make up for the sacrifices which have been entailed on her through twenty years of disquiet due to the guilty machinations of ambitious neighbours; she has need of them in order to stanch the wounds to which the vices of a defective administration are not foreign; she has need of them, in the last place,

---

* The Turkish Admiralty, where the late Conference was held.

in order to develop the reparatory institutions which her new Sovereign has just bestowed on her.

The subjoined brief collection of papers will serve better than long arguments to determine exactly the spirit which must have animated the representatives of the Porte at the Conference. The praiseworthy efforts of the delegates from Europe to ensure a conciliatory solution found, it is clear, a sympathetic and grateful response at Constantinople. How comes it then that the labours of diplomacy have not yet borne conciliatory fruit? This is a complicated question, to which we could only reply by opening up a long discussion. And the work we are now undertaking is not argumentative; it is a work of pure demonstration. It is not our aim to analyse the reasons whereby the negotiations, past and future, may lead to war or to peace. Our prayers are all for peace; but war, disappointing our wishes and our hopes, may from one moment to another rear its horrid head and overshadow the whole world.

The world then ought to know the causes which have produced war, and may have rendered it inevitable. To set forth these causes is the object of the present pamphlet. In other words we propose here to draw up the BALANCE SHEET OF RESPONSIBILITIES.

II.

The Porte, it is said, is responsible for the present situation. Having been admitted twenty years ago into the European family of nations, Turkey has not done what she ought to raise her population to the level of civilized peoples; she has neglected to provide them with institutions calculated to preserve them from those periodical commotions which are a permanent danger for Europe. Let it be so. We admit all the more readily that reproach, since, so far as it was merited, the Ottoman people has taken upon itself to remove it. In one never-to-be-forgotten day the people arose, calm as a judge, and at its powerful breath a throne, whose basis had been undermined by flattery from within, and artificial props from without, fell.

What more can be said? Is it necessary, after this declaration, to discuss the *quantum* of the defects of the previous administration? To do so would be superfluous. We give plenty of tether to the detractors of Turkey; we acknowledge that the Empire has had its period of vicious government, a period when great patriots and perhaps even men of genius were required to accomplish, with the fewest possible shocks, the economico-politico social evolution whose time was due. It is true that the administration was defective; it is true that the men who were chosen by the Sovereign from motives of favour, rather than for their merits, were often wanting in enlightenment, in experience, and in the other qualities which go to make up an able administrator. All this is true, we admit it; but the defects of these men were negative defects; their incapacity might prolong the unsatisfactory situation of the country, impede progress; it had nothing in common with the system of active wrong which tends to arouse popular indignation and to provoke revolt. Let us be forgiven for using a very homely expression, but one which exactly fits our thought: these ill-chosen administrators may have been *stupid*; no one will venture to say they were wicked. Now it is acts of cruel oppression which drive a people to rebellion, and not acts of administrative mismanagement, such as Ottoman functionaries were wont to commit under the late reign. What exasperates a population to the point of insurrectional explosion are the deliberately cruel orders sometimes issued by government functionaries drunk with a sense of authority, and which a soldiery, drunk with alcohol, carries out in a spirit yet more cruel. For example, it was the wanton butchery of the peaceable inhabitants of Warsaw in their churches which provoked the Polish insurrection of 1862-1863. "Could it have been imagined" says an Englishman, an eye-witness of that massacre, "that the Christian 'Governor of a Christian town should give orders 'to trample down a Christian population, an in- 'offensive people, because it enters the house of 'God, or approaches it?"*

We defy any body to state that any Governor in the Ottoman provinces has provoked the passions of the people by acts like this. Who in Turkey has ever entertained the thought of opposing the

---

* Letters addressed to EARL RUSSELL by G. MITCHELL, concerning the events of the 15th October.

free exercise of religious worship, and the free use of the language of the conquered populations? Who would dare, in the 13th century of the Hegira, to do the contrary of what the great Khalif Omar did at Jerusalem, hardly three years after the death of the Prophet? No: whatever faults may be attributed to Ottoman administration it cannot be shown that those faults have been of a nature to cause the insurrectionary facts from which the present phase of the Eastern question has originated. It is, then, elsewhere than in the internal government of the country that the cause of those facts is to be sought. It is elsewhere, too, that the responsibility of them is to be laid.

III.

After the war of 1870-1871 there took place at Constantinople a displacement of influences. The enemies of Turkey came to understand that the hour approached when they might begin serious action The reader may judge of this fact by the care with which the subjoined confidential letter, addressed to Mr. Y...... at Vienna, by Mr. X...... under date of Pera, Constantinople,

March 4th, 1871, touches a little on every subject: politics, administration, religion, men and things:

No. 1.

' The very interesting information which Y. X.
' has been good enough to give me respecting the
' relations of the Prince of Montenegro with our
' Consul at Ragusa, has given me the greatest
' pleasure. Our friends at St. Petersburg can now
' judge of the difference there is between Mr.
' Yonine and Petrovich, and they will understand
' at last how important it is to us to have near
' Prince Nicholas an able functionary with affable
' and distinguished manners calculated to win the
' attachment of everybody.

' The details you give me concerning your
' relations with Khalil Bey, and the intimate ties
' existing between him and the famous Saxon
' statesman, do not astonish me at all. I have
' known your colleague of Turkey for many years.
' Once upon a time, before he had any idea of
' becoming a great man, he liked Russia, as much,
' that is to say, as an Osmanli can like us. Since
' his departure from St. Petersburg, and his political

'alliance with Mustafa Nazyl, he has broken off
'completely from his former friends, and he now
'honours us with his unceasing dislike. There is
'nothing wonderful therefore in the fact that
'Khalil Bey should, as soon as he arrived at
'Vienna, have acquired the friendship of M. de
'Beust. The latter, as an avowed enemy of
'Slavism, could not have found a more active
'auxiliary in his intrigues than Khalil Bey. But
'it is sad to see your colleague of Turkey who,
'thinking to evade the danger, intrigues against
'us, and will end by precipitating his country into
'a deep abyss.

'Thanks to the obstinacy of the Turks, and to
'the self-will of the Patriarch, the breach between
'the Bulgarians and the Greeks has become in-
'evitable. In truth, there was a moment when I
'feared that a reconciliation would be effected;
'but, the Patriarch being inflexible, the affair has
'become so envenomed that all the efforts of Aali
'Pasha will prove fruitless. It is now that our
'activity should be redoubled. If the Vizier
'accepts the Patriarch's resignation (which is
'almost certain), it will be necessary to inaugurate

'the installation of the new Prelate by an address
'from the inhabitants of Thrace, Macedonia, Bosnia,
'and Herzegovina, who will demand national
'bishops. In this way, with each new Patriarch
'we shall gain some dioceses. I have already
'written in this sense to Adrianople and Monastir.
'Your Committee must do the same for Herze-
'govina and Bosnia.

'Have you received the new strategical maps
'of the Western provinces of Turkey? I see by
'the reports of our explorers that we have made
'good progress in working on the feelings of the
'populations, and that even the Mussulmans are
'ready to help us in our task of emancipation.
'Thank God, all is going on well; but I shall be
'still better satisfied when I get orders to ask for
'my passport.'

(Translated from the Russian.)

We shall abstain for the present from any attempt to appreciate this document, whose importance is self-evident. Similar opportunities of exercising the critical faculties of our readers will not, moreover, be wanting in the course of these pages. Our object in reproducing the above letter is to dispense with the necessity of ourselves setting forth the general position of affairs at the period in question, that is to say, at the conclusion of the Franco-German War. This document will serve instead, and it has the advantage over anything we could say in point of actuality and exactness of detail.

Thus, at the beginning of the year 1871 a breach had been produced between the Greek and the Bulgarian Churches. There was, in truth, *a moment when it might have been feared that a reconciliation would be effected;* but happily the Patriarch of Constantinople is a venerable Pontiff, incapable of deserting the principles upon which his Church is founded; and therefore he will not yield. It is clear meanwhile that reconciliation is only possible on condition that he bow to the dissidents. The system, it will be observed, is always the same. At the present time again it is not the insurrection which must yield; it is legitimate authority which must capitulate; peace can only be had at that price. There will then be no reconciliation, for the writer of the letter is sure of his dissidents, and *the efforts of Aali Pasha will prove fruitless.* To any one who can read history, or who has studied Turkey of late years, the whole history of the Eastern crisis is embodied in the eight words which we have underlined above. The efforts of the Grand Vizier, whoever he might be, and of his subordinates of every degree *proved fruitless.* In politics as in matters religious, administrative, and financial, the result was—*Nothing!* A vast intrigue, enveloping the whole country, was incessantly at work, paralyzing its every source of vitality.

In the meanwhile the general plan of the campaign is frankly displayed; the writer of the letter pours out his soul without reserve into the soul of his correspondent. We must, he says, *redouble our activity.* It is necessary that Thrace, Macedonia, Bosnia, and Herzegovina be incited to break away from the Patriarchate, and that, at every change of Patriarch, some dioceses be won over to the cause of the conspirators. Measures have already been taken by the writer as to *Adrianople* and *Monastir.* It is for the Vienna Committee to commence the agitation in *Herzegovina* and in *Bosnia.*

And what about the *strategical maps?* and

about the *explorers* who work upon the *feelings* of the *populations?* How all this smells of the powder that will be burnt in Herzegovina, and of the fumes of the cannibal feats which will be held in Bulgaria by provoking there, in default of an efficacious insurrection, reprisals which will be turned to account in a future *atrocitist* campaign. Yes, you see, all is going on well, *thank God!* Providence, however, has yet a prayer to grant; a last joy is still wanting to our conspirator-diplomatist: *his passport.* "Conspirator-diplomatist!" an odd assortment of words! Has the law of nations then no longer any meaning? Is diplomatic inviolability no longer anything at Constantinople but a discreet mantle destined to conceal great crimes within its folds?

IV.

We have said that Constantinople had become the den of a conspiracy whose outcome was the INSURRECTION OF HERZEGOVINA, and the events which have been called the BULGARIAN MASSACRES. This truth will be proved to demonstration on a perusal of the documents further on. The following points will be established:—

That personages invested with a high diplomatic mandate organised and directed the plot;

That all the Consuls under their orders had, to use a homely phrase, "a finger in the pie," and presided over the work of carrying the plot into execution;

That a powerful affiliation of secret societies, having their organised head abroad, enlaced Turkey and her neighbours in a close net;

That these societies corresponded with Ambassadors, issued orders to Consuls, and obeyed the behests of Princes;

That, lastly, the operations of these societies had for their field not only the European provinces of Turkey, but also those in Asia, and even in Africa.

The above points being made clear, what we have called *the balance of responsibilities* will be self-determined, and the world will know whom it is to reproach for the disquiet from which it is suffering, and the evils which it apprehends.

No. 2.

Mr. X . . .

Pera, Constantinople, 14/26 Nov., 1872.

To Mr. Y . . . at Vienna,

'I wrote to you lately regarding the new
'intrigues of our dear co-religionists. The Phana-
'riotes, after compelling their Patriarch to launch
'their thunders against the Slavic world, are now
'doing all they can to cast out of the Church the
'venerable Prelate who so worthily occupies the
'Patriarchal throne at Jerusalem. Enchanted to
'find an ally worthy of their cause in the person of
'the famous Khalil-Sherif, they have conceived
'the ingenious idea of putting seals on the
'Patriarch Cyril's property at Constantinople. It
'is needless to say that I have taken precautions
'against this new act of Greco-Turkish justice. I
'wrote immediately to C . . . . . to work upon
'the Arabs and urge them to protest against the
'illegal decision of the Phanariote Synod at
'Jerusalem. At the same time I wrote to St.
'Petersburg, and I trust my old plan will at last
'be put into execution, that is to say, to sequester

'the large property which the Church of Jerusalem
'possesses in Russia.

'You see, my dear friend, that my position here
'is not very enviable. If the present *régime* lasts
'some months longer our interests will be gravely
'compromised, and we shall perhaps be obliged to
'give up the Exarchate in order to avoid sacrifices
'yet greater. What a misfortune that our Synod
'did not accept, three years ago, the convocation of
'the Œcumenical Council! The majority of voices
'being secured to us, we could have avoided the
'Schism, and have forced the Greeks to make
'concessions. But who could then have foreseen
'the obstinacy of the Patriarch? It is true, how-
'ever, that the fault is not his, and that he would
'be ready to give in to-day, were he not forced on
'by the *grammarians*, that standing scourge of
'Byzantium.

'The only hope which remains to us is in
'the Ministerial changes which everybody expects
'with the Baïram.

'Our friend A. and the good V. S. are actively
'at work at this. If we succeed, Byzantium will
'see within its walls a new *Millet-Bashi*, and the

'Greek Patriarch will again hold out his hand for 'Panslavic alms.'

(Extract of a private letter translated from Russian.)

Those who know the man and his style will recognise in this epithet "dear" an irony quite *sui generis*. So then, his *dear* Phanariote co-religionists make "new intrigues;" that is to say, that, faithful to the rights of their Church, they are indignant that Mgr. Cyril, Patriarch of Jerusalem, should desire to place his own under obedience to the Metropolitan of Moscow, in consequence of which the "Phanariote" Synod of the Holy City deposes the spiritual chief who thus squanders his pontifical independence. But all is not yet lost. "The Arabs" will be worked upon, and St. Petersburg will "sequester" the property of the unruly Church.

There is, however, a drawback to this. The Synod of Moscow made a mistake in rejecting the convocation of the Œcumenical Council! It would have been easy to contrive a majority, and to have thus remained masters of the situation; whereas here was a somewhat troublesome schism; this might lead to a declaration of heresy against the Bulgarian Church, and even the Russian Church. In such case, how would it be possible to follow up the idea of *Russifying all the Eastern Churches?* Decidedly then, this schism was a mishap; but who could have foreseen that Mgr. Anthimos would refuse " Panslavic money"? Happily our friend A. . . . , who can boast of nothing Patriarchal in his person or his life, albeit his name corresponds with that of a great Patriarch, does not show the same aversion to the roubles of Panslavism; nor does the good V. S., very great lady and mother of the grand Signor as she is, scruple to defile her fingers with Muscovite gold. So long as these worthy servants of foreign intrigue " work actively," there is still hope for the good cause.

No. 3.

Mr. X. . . .
Pera, Constantinople, 23rd Nov.
(5th Dec.) 1872.
To Mr. Y. . . . at Vienna.

'The Baïram has changed nothing in the pro-
'visional state of things which I spoke of in my

'last letter. Notwithstanding all that persons of
'sound and enlightened minds could do, the clique
'of intriguers has carried the day, and our *petit
'crevé de Paris* remains as before at the head of the
'foreign affairs of the poor sick man, whom we
'are trying to cure in spite of himself.

'It would be useless to give you all the details
'of the struggle we have had to sustain against
'Midhat's party, protected as it is by my western
'colleagues. You will ask me, perhaps, whence
'comes this infatuation of the Western Ambassadors
'for a statesman who is the true representative of
'the Turkish *ancien régime*, and has not the slightest
'tie with European civilization, of which my col-
'leagues would have it appear they are the
'disinterested protectors in our chaotic east. The
'sympathy with which they honour him comes
'simply from the fact that Midhat carries his hos-
'tility to Russia to the verge of absurdity. The
'cruelty of which he gave proofs when in Bulgaria—
'a matter for which I certainly cannot blame him, so
'far as the interests of the government he served
'are considered—is the chief reason of the popu-
'larity which he has acquired in certain embassies.

'It is thanks to these considerations that Khalil
'too continues to be in the good graces of my
'colleagues, and that he has managed to retain his
'place for the present, in spite of the just indigna-
'tion of the Sultan against his giddy minister. The
'latter, instead of serving the true interests of the
'country of his adoption, does nothing but commit
'folly upon folly, and that solely in order to spite
'the sovereign of his native country and our
'brothers by race, It is but lately that M. Christich
'confided to me that it has become almost
'impossible for him to protect the interests of his
'country against the ill-will of a minister animated
'as Khalil is, by the most hostile feelings towards
'the Slavs. Having surrounded himself with
'persons belonging to the very famous 'Young
'Turkey' party, and with Poles who have again
'come flocking in like crows to the quarry, he stirs
'up under hand the 'Old Phanariotes,' and makes
'impossible any compromise between the Greeks
'and Bulgarians. It is true at the same time that
'the fanatics of the Patriarchate make his task an
'easy one. Those degenerate descendants of John
'Chrysostom are delighted at having found a pro-

'tector who can enter into the spirit of their
'intrigues. I have written lately to our consuls
'to cease giving subsidies and assistance to the
'Greek churches and schools. Perhaps by this
'means their eyes will be opened, and the sheep
'who have lost their way through the Phanariote
'propaganda will return to the fold.

'As to the Bulgarians I cannot sufficiently
'commend their tact and *savoire faire*. They
'have thoroughly understood the advice I gave
'them through O . . u, and they behave in a way
'which puts their enemies at a loss for any accusa-
'tion against them to the Government

'I received yesterday a letter from Prince
'Nicholas, who informs me of the bad state of his
'affairs in Albania. As you will see by the
'enclosed copy, he unfortunately says nothing
'regarding the consequences of the arrests effected
'by Shevket. Has he written anything to you on
'that subject? Mr. H. . . . reports that the
'Agents of the Prince lately dispatched to Scutari
'have had to return at once to Cettigné, for fear
'of being arrested by the police. Have you no
'means of arranging this affair with your com-

' mittee, and of pointing out to it the line of action
' it must take in the event of its proving impos-
' sible for Montenegro to maintain her agents in
' Albania. Be so good as to let me know what
' you have done on this head. . . . .

(Extract of a letter translated from Russian.)

So then, persons of "sound and enlightened minds" wished to cure the "poor sick man;" the "clique of intriguers" objected to this. Three years later, when these same *intriguers* had already long been laid on the official shelf, the "sound minds" had free scope to apply their regimen. The desired result was soon obtained: A dose of Herzegovina, a drop of Bosnia, a grain of Bulgaria, a dram of Servia and Montenegro, sufficed to bring the patient into the satisfactory state so much desired by his good friends the Slavo-Russians. Is it not perfectly "ridiculous," too, in Midhat Pasha to be hostile to Russia? In sober truth, if that statesman had not given proof, during the first Bulgarian insurrection, of a degree of severity which the writer of the above letter has chosen to term *cruelty*, it would have been a dishonour to him. But there is always a grain of sympathy in every true Muscovite heart for energetic acts even where they are, by straining the note, designated as acts of cruelty;—because, to be sure, so much of that sort of thing had to be resorted to in Poland and elsewhere. On the other hand, it is very clear that the same statesman who has been guilty of giving serious thought to a constitutional *régime* and the liberties of the people cannot "have the slightest tie with European civilization." The proper way is to keep promising constitutions, as has been done in Poland; but one must take care not to grant them, if one would have anything in common with a civilized statesman. Learn this principle, Your Highness, or make up your mind to be a barbarian for ever.

And what shall we say about that other would-be civilized statesman, the " Khalil " who ventures to " spite the brothers by race " of the illustrious diplomatist-conspirator ? Can one conceive a Turkish minister of state guilty of the " folly " of being " animated by the most hostile feelings towards the Slavs." And the Poles, those " crows flocking into the quarry,"—just like the Cossacks do when they fall upon a Ruthene town !—What audacity!—As for the "Old Phanariotes" but one method remains to be tried in order to awaken them to a sense of shame, and that is, to cut off the supplies from their churches and schools.

But when we come to the Bulgarians, what tact they have, and how readily they listen to Mr. O . . u! On the other hand, Prince * * * * is put out. Shevket Pasha has had the bad taste to lock up the emissaries sent by His Highness to raise disturbances in Albania! The Vienna Committee ought really to take measures for protecting the Prince and his agents from such outrages!

No. 4.

Mr. X . . .

Pera, Constantinople, 27 Nov. (9 Dec.) 1872.

To Mr. Y . . . at Vienna.

'Mehmed Rushdi Pasha has again fallen under
' the pernicious influence of the Minister of Foreign
' Affairs. Ever since his advent to power, that
' statesman has been leaning now to one side and
' now to the other; but he has at length given
' himself over body and soul to the interest of the
' Magyarophile policy of Khalil & Co.

'You have no doubt heard of the compliments
'which the Sultan has thought proper to make to
'his Sadrazam at the Baïram audience. These
'compliments, spread far and wide by the Young
'Turkey party and its adherents, the Grœculi of the
'Phanar, have produced a most painful impression
'upon that part of the population of Stamboul
'which knows how to appreciate at their true value
'the pompous promises of Khalil and Austro-
'Hungarian humbug.'

'The consolidation of Khalil's power has had
'as its first consequence, the recrudescence of the
'Greek attacks against the Patriarch of Jerusalem
'and the Bulgarian Exarch. These two prelates,
'who will probably fall, thanks to their devotion
'to our interests, are the object of so many attacks,
'that I admire the patience with which they are
'borne. Mgr. Anthimos in particular, who could
'if he chose, stir up against the Porte very grave
'difficulties, conducted himself in an admirable
'manner. After the outrage which the very
'perspicacious Turco-Egyptian diplomatist lately
'inflicted on him, he has had the wisdom to con-
'form exactly to the line of conduct which I had

'traced out for him. For the rest, he will not
'have to wait long, for, with the fitful and pas-
'sionate character of the Sultan the present order
'of things cannot be expected to last more than
'two, or at most, three months longer.

'As regards Mgr. Cyril, his position is much
'more serious. If the Porte sanctions his deposi-
'tion the Synod of Jerusalem will forthwith
'proceed to the election of a new Patriarch, and
'thus shall we be frustrated of our rights over the
'Holy Sepulchre. In order to obviate such a
'disaster, I have written to P. . . . , C. . . . ,
'and Y. . . . , to agitate dextrously among the
'population of Syria and Palestine for the creation
'of an Arab Church, independent of the Pa-
'triarchate, and which would elect for its chief,
'Mgr. Cyril.

'Khalil does not confine himself to ecclesi-
'astical agitation. He has just had recourse to
'another device which will give you an idea of
'his friendship for us. The news of the robbery
'of the Roustchouk post has suggested to him
'the ingenious idea of throwing the responsibility

'of that act upon the Bulgarians, whom he is now
'endeavouring to persuade His Majesty are the
'most dangerous enemies of the Empire. You
'cannot imagine the annoyance this news has given
'me. Thanks to the stupidity of our M. . . . .
'one of the persons who took part in that act of
'brigandage, happens to have been affiliated by
'our agency at Roustchouk. If the Turkish police
'should arrest this individual, I fear revelations
'which cannot but do us the greatest harm. I am
'surprised that so sensible a man as Mr. M. . . .
'can have associated with our cause a person
'whose antecedents he was ignorant of. This
'unpardonable fault should serve as a lesson
'to us; and in fact, I have already acted upon
'it by instructing all our consuls to abstain
'henceforth from affiliating anybody without
'previous sanction from me.

'I learn that Khalil has proposed to Mehmed-
'Rushdi that the too famous hangman-in-chief,
'Midhat, should be sent to Sofia as President of
'the Committee of Inquiry. Here we are then,
'on the eve of new exploits by this terrible hero of

'bloody assizes, who assuredly will not let slip
'such an opportunity of expediting *ad patres* some
'hundreds of unfortunate *ghiaours*!'

'Very many thanks for the most interesting
'details you give me regarding the Tcheque
'struggle. What a misfortune, however, that this
'cause, so noble in principle, should not have been
'preserved from the intrigues of new Judases!
'The example of Sabina has, unhappily, found
'imitators, and this cannot fail to compromise the
'the most sacred of causes.'

(Extract of a letter translated from Russian.)

He was in a very bad humour, our amiable diplomatist-conspirator, on this 27th November (9th December), and not without reason. The Sultan has so far forgotten himself as to address a compliment to his anti-slavic minister! The cabinet is now invested with the style and title of a commercial firm, and appears as "Khalil & Co." In the same way the "Old Phanariotes" and the "grammarians" now degenerate into "Grœculi." As to the policy of Count Andrassy, the style in which it is characterised may be thought by some pure Tartar—"Austro-Hungarian humbug" is at any rate not very diplomatic—but then, why do people thus persist in crossing Your Excellency? On that day nearly everything went wrong in a most provoking way, even to the associate of " your Roustchouk agency" who takes it into his head to take part in the robbery of the Post. Were he to be arrested and to make revelations, what a mess! However, some good is to be got out of every evil. That highway robber to whom you have become affiliated, one does not exactly know how, will at any rate serve as a caution against such awkwardnesses for the future, and there will be this advantage to Your Excellency, that nobody henceforward must be affiliated " without your previous sanction." This same 27th November (9th December) was an unlucky day for you even in the matter of the " too-famous hangman-in-chief" who did not after all accord you the satisfaction of sending *ad patres* some hundreds of honest people; for he preferred indulging in his constitutional *rêveries* at home to accepting that mission. And Mgr. Anthimos, that prelate " so devoted to your interests!" And Mgr. Cyril whose deposition may have the effect of " frustrating you of your rights over the Holy

Sepulchre!" Lastly, to crown this series of misfortunes, in Bohemia the Tcheque cause refuses to prosper just as if it were not " the most sacred of causes." Certainly Your Excellency must have felt that the 27th November (9th December) was quite an unlucky day. Happily there remained the solace of "agitating dextrously" in Syria and Palestine. This was something after all.

No. 5.

Mr. X . . .

Pera, Constantinople, 7/19th Dec.

To Mr. Y . . . at Vienna.

'The Greeks decidedly do not intend to remain
'quiet. Since the advent to power of their sorry
'protector, they dabble in such a quagmire of
'intrigues that one must be as blind and obstinate
'an enemy of the truth as Khalil to continue to
'put faith in the lies which are daily put forth by
'his friends the *sarafs* and orators of the Phanar.'

'Thanks to the perfidious insinuations of these
'miserable Galata stock-jobbers, the orthodox East
'is about to lose the eminent prelate who is the
'glory of our Church; and, what is yet more sad,

'here are the Greeks, those boasted friends of
'liberty, imploring the protection of the Austrians
'and Prussians, and soliciting the intervention of
'Protestants in their ecclesiastical affairs, whilst
'refusing the right to do so to their co-religionist,
'Russia. Their rage has been still more heightened
'against us at the news of the sequestration of the
'conventual property in Bessarabia. This loss is
'so material a one for the Phanariote prelates that
'I would be ready to wager we should soon see
'the old men of the Synod prostrate themselves
'before us, acknowledging their *culpa*, were it not
'that they stand in fear of the "grammarians" of
'Galata! It is these last, supported by some
'banker-orators and by the scribblers in the *Neologos*
'and the *phare du Bosphore*, who keep alive the
'flame of discord.

'The only thing which might put an end to
'this melancholy reign of intrigues would be a
'change of ministry, or at any rate the removal of
'Khalil, who alone has an interest in all these
'religious dissentions. I just learn from the Palace
'that it is by no means improbable we may before
'long be delivered from this incorrigible mischief-

'maker! The old and faithful friend of the most
'estimable mother of Madame Novikow has also
'lately promised Madame I......ff to act in that
'sense at the Palace...'

(Letter translated from Russian.)

The survivors of the old Midhat ministry certainly had the merit of putting our diplomatist beside himself. The whole Greek population of Constantinople are now angrily stigmatised as "miserable Galata stock-jobbers." On the other hand, the Patriarch whom the Synod of Jerusalem has judged unworthy to remain at its head is styled "the eminent Prelate who is the glory of our"— that is, the Russian—"church." Passion blinds one, truly. Here is a most able diplomatist, and yet one who cannot understand that a prelate who is the glory of the Russian Church, must necessarily be the shame of the Greek Church, which is now fully alive to Russian designs against Hellenism, with respect to matters ecclesiastical as well as secular. But for all that, if he is carried away by his feelings as a man, as a diplomatist he does not lose his head. The Ministry must be made to fall; he must gain this point even if it be necessary to use the good offices of ladies. These last he does not hesitate to name at full length, except in the instance of "the old and faithful friend of the most estimable mother of Madame Novikow." We humbly confess that the cypher in our possession has failed to furnish us the key to this mysterious reference.

No. 6.

Mr. Z . . .

St. Petersburg, 8/20th December, 1872.

To Mr. Y . . . at Vienna.

'As General Ignatieff keeps you informed of
'all that passes at Constantinople it would be
'superfluous for me to repeat to you the dishearten-
'ing accounts which we receive from Tzargrad.
'The advent to power of Khalil Pasha certainly
'was not calculated to give us the hope of regain-
'ing the influence which we lost through the fall
'of Mahmoud Pasha.

'You will easily perceive by the General's
'letters that he always retains that optimism which
'marks his character. For my own part I will
'frankly own to you that I no longer believe in the
'brilliant expectations of our friends at Constanti-

'nople. The Anglo-Austrian intrigue is so power-
'ful at Constantinople that I no longer hope for
'the speedy return to power of Mahmoud, the more
'especially since the Sultan himself, with his weak
'and vacillating character, seems to have allowed
'himself to be persuaded that it is necessary to
'maintain the present ministry in power.

'Prince Gortchakoff has just written to the
'General to suspend for sometime all attacks
'against the Minister of Foreign Affairs and the
'Grand Vizier. Khalil's character and the state
'of feeling in Turkey enable us to foresee that
'some favourable circumstance must shortly arise
'which by proving the incompetency of these two
'statesmen, will oblige the Sultan to confide the
'administration of affairs once more to our friends.

'In the meanwhile we are of opinion that it
'would be useful to prepare the ground in quite a
'different way. As Montenegro and Servia may
'obtain for us the opportunity we are looking for,
'you will devote your attention to those two
'countries. By favouring the material and moral
'development of those two advanced posts of
'Slavism, we shall be serving our cause much more

'effectually than by palace intrigues unworthy of our great country and the idea it represents.

'You have no doubt learnt the latest decision regarding the sequestration of the property of the Church of Jerusalem. Though it comes rather late, this measure will not be the less salutary in its effects upon our religious adversaries. The Greeks, it is to be hoped, will understand the insanity of their attacks against Russia and the Bulgarians, especially when they see the Œcumenical Patriarchal Throne, of which they are so proud, depending upon the benevolence of a Khalil, who, in order to satisfy his rancour, keeps urging them against us."

(Letter translated from Russian.)

People at St. Petersburg see things more clearly than they do at Constantinople, and Mr. Z . . . sneers at the optimism of Mr. X . . . Upon the whole there is a little more dignity in the above letter than in the preceding ones. The palace intrigues are pronounced "unworthy," and a preference is expressed for operations on the side of Servia and Montenegro, "those two advanced posts of Slavism." It is indeed from those quarters that the road must be opened which leads to the conquest of *Tzargrad*, " the CITY of the TZARS.":—such is the name which the Slavs already give to the Turkish capital.

Mr. Z . . . , it must be owned, too readily allows himself to be discouraged. Why so soon despair of the "return to power of Mahmoud"? Make your minds easy, good doctors of the " poor sick man," Mahmoud will come back in due time, and through him you will have the satisfaction of arousing European opinion, by means of the *iradé* of October.

No. 7.

Mr. X . . .

Pera, Constantinople, 13/25 Dec., 1872.

To Mr. Y . . . at Vienna.

' Khalil Pasha has kept his word well! He had
' promised Mgr. Anthimos to give his attention
' after the Baïram to the Greco-Bulgarian question,
' and he has done so after his fashion.

' Having been invited by the Grand Vizier to
' call upon the Minister of Foreign Affairs in order

'to set forth the wishes of the Bulgarian com-
'munity, the Exarch was received by Khalil
'Pasha in a manner worthy of that statesman.
'Instead of listening to the explanations and
'wishes of the venerable prelate, the Ottoman
'Minister declared to him, with the greatest
'haughtiness, that the Porte had decided to annul
'the firman promulgated under Aali, since the
'relations between the Orthodox and the Bulgarian
'Churches are no longer the same as formerly.
'Neither the respectful observations of Mgr.
'Anthimos, nor his protestations, having had any
'effect in shaking Khalil's resolve, the Exarch had
'to leave the presence of the Minister, carrying
'with him the conviction that the greatest of
'iniquities was soon to be consummated.

'According to the information I receive, Khalil
'wishes to annul the former firman, and to sub-
'stitute another for it, recognizing the Bulgarians
'officially as schismatics who are thrust out of
'the pale of Orthodoxy. I confess I did not know
'Khalil in this new capacity until now. So then,
'we must add to all the others in which he has
'already been recognized, the quality of a profound

'theologian, and an authority in matters of dogma.
'That he should venture to pronounce a decision
'on a purely Christian dogmatic point is such an
'utter absurdity that I would refuse to believe the
'fact had I not been, so to say, a witness of the
'theological prowess of the Reverend Father
'Khalil.

'I am very curious to see how he will decide
'on the incident which will before long happen in
'the Church of Antioch. Thanks to our relations
'with the Primates and Prelates of that Patri-
'archate, the Synod of Antioch will infallibly
'repeat the history enacted at Jerusalem, with this
'difference, that the Patriarch will be disavowed
'by his Synod for having declared against us.
'We shall see how the learned Turco-Egyptian
'will demean himself under these circumstances.*

'It is needless to tell you that the affair of
'Antioch will not stand alone: Roustchouk, Viddin,
'Varna, and other Bulgarian towns will soon give
'signs of life, and the local authorities will have to
'reckon with the effervescence provoked by the

---

* The Synod of Antioch disappointed the hopes of the fomenters of dissension.

'inexpressible partiality of Young Turkey. I have
'already given my instructions on this head to our
'consuls and agents, who will have to abstain from
'any ostensible intervention. Who laughs longest
'will laugh best.'

(Letter translated from Russian.)

He who has "laughed longest" is doubtless the one who has had an interest in rejoicing over the frightful misfortunes which have happened in Bulgaria, and the consequences they produced, through the management of operators so clever as those "consuls" who were "instructed to abstain from any ostensible intervention." In reading phrases like this, one fancies the documents in which they are contained are not letters written in a diplomatic residence, but extracts from the archives of a secret police office.

No. 8.

Mr. X . . .

Pera, Constantinople, 28 Dec. (9 Jan.) 1872.

To Mr. Y . . . at Vienna.

'You have no doubt read in our newspapers
'here, and especially in those published in Turkish,

'that the Porte, taking into consideration the
'armaments which have been going on for some
'time past in Servia, has instructed the governors
'of the frontier provinces towards that principality,
'and the commandants of the troops in garrison
'in those parts to hold themselves prepared for any
'eventuality. This news, and the rumours of con-
'siderable armaments in Turkey, have obliged the
'Servian government to address to the Porte a de-
'mand for explanations. In reply to M. Christich's
'inquiries, Khalil Pasha stated that all these
'rumours were without foundation, and that the
'Government would cause them to be officially
'contradicted.'

'Notwithstanding this reply of the Minister
'and the official contradiction, the Servians certainly
'will not be re-assured as to the warlike tendencies
'of the present Ministry. The Sultan's Govern-
'ment, which appears to receive pretty correct
'information of all that passes in Servia and the
'Slavic Provinces in the north-west of the Empire,
'does all it can not to be taken unawares.'

'I have lately ascertained that the Porte, fearing
'a speedy explosion of the discontent which it

'unceasingly provokes by its silly policy, wishes to
'open a campaign before the Servians are ready to
'undertake the realisation of their projects. Khalil
'and his friends think that the Servians, when
'once chastised as the Greeks were in the matter
'of Crete, would become as submissive and servile
'as the Hellenes. . One must belong to the con-
'ceited clique of 'Young Turkey' to be able to
'suppose that the Servians are as cowardly as the
'Greeks. It is to be hoped that the eyes of these
'gentlemen will soon be opened; but, please God,
'it will be a little too late for the dear sick man!

'The Greek papers have not deceived you in
'notifying so pompously the conversion of Mon-
'sieur C. . . . (or G. . . . Effendi, in official
'language). I am, however, in a position to re-
'assure you on this head. If Mr. C. . . . has re-
'entered the pale of the Church so unworthily
'presided over by the Patriarch Anthimos, that step
'must not be attributed to his personal repentance
'nor to his conviction of the injustice of the cause
'represented by the Exarch. Mr. C. . . . has
'been obliged to return within the Phanariote fold,
'in the first place through the insinuations of his

'wife, a Greek by birth and conviction, and next
'by pecuniary considerations, so powerful in those
'quarters. Occupying as he does a somewhat
'important post in the service of the Porte,
'Mr. C. . . . was simply afraid of finding himself
'calumniated by the Greeks, and of losing his
'salary (about 8,000 roubles) in consequence. This
'gentleman who enjoys, justly enough, great con-
'sideration among his fellow countrymen, has taken
'part in, or let it rather be said, has secretly di-
'rected the whole course of the Bulgarian negotia-
'tions. This will suffice to give you a correct
'estimate of the sincerity of his conviction.'

(Private letter translated from Russian.)

Not so silly as your Excellency is pleased to call it, the policy which consists in being pretty correctly informed of all that passes in Servia and the Slavic provinces of the Empire, and which desired to open a campaign before the Servian projects could be realized. Fortunately you were awake, you and the lady whom you lately designated as the " old and faithful friend of the most estimable mother of Madame Novikow;" and you two together, no doubt, took measures to prevent its being possible to judge whether the Servians could become as " servile" and as " cowardly" as the Greeks. Only in that way could it be contrived that the matter should not be put to the proof before it would be " a little too late for the dear sick man." As regards the personage whose name we abstain from giving as you do at full length, and to whom the Porte seems to have the weakness of assigning a salary equivalent to 8,000 roubles, we perfectly understand that what you consider as an act of apostacy in him, should not provoke the feelings of religious indignation, usually so ticklish. For, did he not " secretly direct the whole course of the Bulgarian negotiations ?" How you must have laughed at the people who were so simple as to be astonished, you being there, at the bloody scenes of which Bulgaria in the end became the theatre !

No. 9.

Mr. X . . .

Pera, Constantinople, 4/16 January, 1873.
To Mr. Y . . . at Vienna.

' The struggle between the Œcumenical Patriarch
' and the Bulgarians has assumed of late a diplo-

'matic character. Whilst the Greeks set on foot
'all the intrigues they can devise in order to com-
'promise the Bulgarians towards the Porte, the
'latter oppose to their adversaries a line of conduct
'full of frankness and of firmness based on the
'consciousness which they have of their strength.
'The demands of the Greeks may be summed up
'under the four following heads:—

'1. Annulment of the Firman decreed under
'Aali, and drawing up of another in which the
'Bulgarians will be declared schismatics.

'2. Change in the costume of the Bulgarian
'clergy.

'3. Maintenance, in the possession of the
'Greeks, of the churches, convents, schools, and
'other public establishments which are situated in
'the provinces having a mixed population.

'4. Maintenance of the right of the Greek
'patriarchate to send its bishops into the Bulgarian
'provinces.

'These rights, which our good friend Khalil
'seems disposed to grant to the Greeks, are so
'contrary to the interests of the Bulgarian Church,
'that the Exarch, notwithstanding his extreme

'repugnance to do so, has been obliged again to
' come forward and combat the intrigues of our
' enemies. It was the day before yesterday that
' Mgr. Anthimos went to see the famous minister,
' who had invited him to go and talk over this
' unfortunate affair. Their interview, however,
' was of short duration, and led to nothing. After
' making a show of politeness and kindliness at
' first, Khalil ended by threats when he found that
' the Exarch was not disposed to yield to the claims
' of the Phanariotes on the smallest point.

  ' The affair of the Exarchate is, moreover, not
' the only one which has gone wrong, thanks to
' the intrigues and vile calumnies of our ex-friends.
' By means of an outcry raised by the Phanariotes
' and their new allies, the scribblers at Vienna, our
' consuls in Macedonia have begun to be crossed in
' a thousand ways. You have no doubt learnt that
' a commission of enquiry has been appointed by
' the Patriarch to proceed to Mount Athos. I
' certainly should not have bestowed any attention
' on these Greco-Turkish machinations had not our
' enemies perfidiously mixed up the names of L . . .
' and J . . . in their calumnies. I have, conse-

'quently, had to write to those gentlemen to quit
'their posts for a time and to come here, after
'having given our friends the necessary instructions
'for nullifying the new Greek intrigues.

'I accept with the greatest gratitude your
'obliging proposal with regard to the *Clio,* and I
'feel certain that the Imperial Ministry will not
'refuse to ratify the promise you have made to the
'excellent editor of that very influential journal.
'For the rest, should the prince still begrudge the
'money, I engage to pay from my own purse the
'5,000 roubles which you have promised to the
'editor of the Trieste paper. The co-operation of
'that journal will be the more useful to us since it
'is looked up to as a great authority among the
'Christian populations of the Turkish provinces,
'and thus the *Clio* will be of more service to us
'than the Bulgarian papers published in Roumania,
'and the small Servian prints.'

(Private letter translated from Russian.)

True, the Bulgarians must have been conscious
of their force, that is to say the force of a great
empire, whose ambitious views they were uncon-
sciously serving. As to the four Greek points, it

was high time to bring about the ministerial change which was destined to consign them to the waste-paper basket. If they had succeeded in being carried out, before six months were over no Bulgarian peasant would have seen a Russian priest without crossing himself as he withdrew to a safe distance. This simple measure would have quashed the Bulgarian question and have made impossible the cold-blooded murders which provoked the massacres of Bazardjik and Batak. It is easy to understand that Russian influence was at work to annihilate the four Greek points. This letter is important too as showing the tip of the cloven hoof as regards Mount Athos. It is a very serious affair that Mount Athos business, although it is one which most people know nothing about. If an end be not put to the Slavic intrigue by means of which the Russian monk is insensibly supplanting the Greek monk, Macedonia will before long become a second Bulgaria. Now, it would seem that the first has already produced calamities enough.

No. 10.

Mr. X . . .

Pera, Constantinople, 8/20 February, 1873.

To Mr. Y . . . at Vienna.

'So here we have a new ministry, although in
'truth it is but a clumsy re-plastering of the old
'one. *Bonnet blanc, blanc bonnet ;* this stereotyped
'phrase expresses the state of things to perfection.

'You no doubt recollect the young aide-de-
'camp whom Fuad Pasha took with him to Syria
'in 1860. Who could then have supposed that
'this young soldier, belonging to an Ottomanised
'Greek family, would be called within thirteen
'years to the first post in the Empire!

'The advent of Essad Pasha demonstrates very
'clearly the force and persistence of the fixed idea
'of the Sultan, the new Ladrazam being greatly
'devoted to Prince Youssouf, and intimately,
'bound up with his interests.

'The dismissal of Mehmet Rushdi was brought
'about independently of any political motives and
'solely through a cabal of the ladies of the Palace,
'who found the young and brilliant general to
'their taste. I cannot therefore, yet forecast the

'nature of my relations with him. What vexes
'me in the meanwhile, is to see. Khalil still in
'possession of his portfolio and thus, although his
'power is greatly shaken, enabled to continue his
'silly intrigues against Slavism.

'This minister last week sent word to the
'Exarch that the Porte was firmly resolved to
'authorise the Patriarchate to send its bishops to
'all the Bulgarian Exarchies. This communication
'so greatly afflicted Mgr. Anthimos that he would
'have fallen ill, had I not endeavoured to reassure
'him with a promise of the decisive support of our
'government. By my advice, he made reply to
'Khalil through the medium of his vicar, that,
'seeing the complaints and protests which were
'reaching him from all the Bulgarian Exarchies, he
'feared that the arrival of Greek bishops would
'create great disorders; and that he consequently
'threw all the responsibility of what might happen
'upon those who, against his advice, might have
'recourse to that measure.

'Our friends at Toultcha have carried out the
'orders we gave them some weeks ago. They have
'got the Bulgarians of Toultcha to sign an address

'to the Metropolitan of Roustchouk protesting
'against the annulment of the Firman. This
'protest has already produced a great impression
'here, and it is to be hoped that this and other
'demonstrations of the same kind which are in
'course of preparation in Bulgaria and Thrace,
'will prevent Khalil from precipitating matters,
'if they do not even have the effect of making him
'lose the seat which he so unworthily occupies at
'the Council of Ministers.

'If these demonstrations do not suffice to give
'us the victory, I shall have recourse to the *ultima*
'*ratio*—the *cotillon*.

'The dust which I have managed to throw into
'the eyes of the commission of enquiry at Roust-
'chouk has succeeded, if not completely, at any
'rate in part. The members of the commission are
'now persuaded that all that affair was got up and
'carried through by the Bulgarian emissaries from
'Bucharest. I trust that in the end it will be
'acknowledged at St. Petersburgh that I was in the
'right, especially when it is seen how easily we
'contrive to save appearances.'

(Translated from Russian.)

In order not to tire the attention of the reader we shall close with the above letter the first series of documents which we have undertaken to present to the public. An instructive lesson is to be derived from it. One sees a personage invested with high functions, and sheltered by diplomatic inviolability, placing at the disposal of an intrigue, a plot, all the powerful elements of action which he owes to his privileged position. He conspires against a friendly Government to which he is accredited. Can there be a more serious crime? Is it not absolutely equivalent to a violation of territory? A soldier passes a frontier with his gun on his shoulder; it suffices to provoke a fearful war between two States. What then should be the consequences of the introduction of an army of foreign agents who come to foment disturbances and lay trains for the explosion of civil war? It is true, as the writer of these letters so *naively* lets us know, that no handle can be obtained against him, "seeing how easily we contrive to save appearances!"

VI.

We have now been let into the intimate confidence of the guiding spirit. Let us next descend a degree in the hierarchy, and watch step by step how the plan of operations has been carried out in its most essential details.

No. 11.

Cyphered dispatch from Mr. . . . Consul at Scutari to the Committee at Vienna, dated 8/20 August, 1872.

'The imprisonment of the Albanians who
' would not, or rather, who could not deliver to the
' Turkish authorities the most influential chiefs
' of the Mirdites, has produced in the country a
' great effervescence, which, I am inclined to
' believe will end by creating an untoward in-
' fluence on the relations of Montenegro with the
' Christians of this province. These last, irritated
' by the ever-increasing oppression of the Turks,
' and observing the apparently impassible de-
' meanour of the Montenegrin Government, which
' they attribute to a sentiment of fear, may become
' reconciled with the Turks, and prove to be as

'exasperated against the Montenegrins as they
'have hitherto been devoted to their interests.

'In order to remedy this state of things as far
'as possible I have sent two of our friends to the
'Mirdites and the neighbouring tribes with
'presents in money and some arms. My agents
'are charged to soothe our allies with promises of
'a speedy solution of their disputes with the
'Turks.

'As regards the policy of Montenegro I have
'recommended my agents to explain to the chief
'Shion that Prince Nicholas is ready to fall upon
'the Turks, and that he is only waiting till the
'latter afford him a plausible pretext for com-
'mencing hostilities.'

(Translated from Russian.)

The above document, like all those which will follow, is full of revelations touching the distribution of arms and money to those destined to rise in revolt. It would fatigue the reader to be stopped at every moment by long critical reflections. We shall therefore confine ourselves to throwing in relief by a few short remarks, the salient points of each dispatch.

There is nothing more remarkable in these documents than the cynicism with which the writers, in the midst of the most overwhelming admissions of the work on which they are engaged, speak as if the agitation which they have exerted themselves to produce is the result of Turkish oppression, and not of their own manœuvres.

No. 12.

Extracts of a cyphered dispatch from Mr. . . . ., Consul at Seraïevo to the Committee at Vienna, dated 10/22 August, 1872.

. . . .

'All these changes have at last completely dis-
'credited the government in the minds of the
'population, who already feel, without any necessity
'to impress it on them, that *deliverance will come*
'*to them from Servia, free and strong through the*
'*support of Russia.*

'The conflict at Kolashin has so alarmed the
'Turks that they have concentrated eight batta-
'lions in the direction of Albania and Herzegovina.
'It remains to be seen, however, whether this
'measure of precaution will suffice to arrest *the*

'*aggressive movements which are in preparation on*
'*both sides.*'

(Translation from Russian).

"The aggressive movements which are in preparation on both sides!" The avowal is one to be remembered, in connection with the idea that "deliverance will come from Servia, free and strong through the support of Russia."

No. 13.

Extract of a cyphered dispatch from Mr. . . . . . Vice-Consul at Mostar to the Committee at Vienna, dated 11/23rd August, 1872.

'The agent whom I sent to Niksich and
'Popovo returned this morning bringing several
'petitions from the inhabitants addressed to the
'Imperial Government.

'After exposing in detail all that they have to
'endure at the hands of the Mussulman authorities
'our co-religionists implore the clemency of *the*
'*Imperial Government*, and ask either to be taken
'into Russia where they may dwell secure from
'persecution, or else the means to fight against the
'enemy of our religion, and to throw off a yoke

'which has become too odious to be any longer
'supportable.

'The *sums of money* which I have sent to the
'relations and friends of Cocacerwich have enabled
'18 of them to proceed to Montenegro and to place
'themselves at the disposal of the Commander of
'the valiant Montenegrin bands. As to the others,
'being unable to leave the country on account of
'their families, they have begged those who went
'to Montenegro to send them, as soon as they can,
'*gunpowder, to enable them to fly to arms at the first
'call of Prince Nicholas.*'

The "*Imperial* Government" here in question is not, as will be understood, that of the legitimate Sovereign of the petitioners; it is to a foreign Sovereign that the populations are incited to address their petitions, and it is the Consul of that foreign Sovereign who corrupts them by distributions of money to enable them to take service in the army of the future enemy of their country!

No. 14.

Extract of a cyphered dispatch from Mr. . . . Consul at Seraïevo to the Committee at Vienna, dated 21st August (2 September), 1872.

'The festival at Belgrade has produced an excellent impression everywhere. The patriots of Seraïevo have been so electrified by it that several notables have come to see me declaring their readiness to devote the half of their fortune for the armament of the volunteers in case of a war between Turkey and Servia.

'Finding them in this frame of mind I have thought myself called upon to congratulate them on their patriotic sentiments, and to promise *that I would inform the Imperial Government* of them. I have endeavoured to soothe their minds with regard to the imminence of war, remarking that if hostilities do not begin now, *that does not mean that they are indefinitely postponed.* . . . 'I explained to them that Servia, which is preparing seriously for an approaching war, will require the co-operation of all her children. You will do well therefore to *carry out your plans of armament.*

'After long discussions which we had together they decided to send two members of their society to Belgrade, to place in Prince Milan's hands the money which they desire *to give to the country.*'

(Translated from Russian.)

The "country" of the Bosniacs is the principality over which reigns he who will one day declare war against their own sovereign; for hostilities are far from being "indefinitely postponed," the Consul has declared it in the paternal discourse made with the view of keeping them "electrified." The foreign "Imperial Government" to whom Europe is indebted for the happy readiness of the populations to revolt, comes in here with an unparalled *à propos*.

No. 15.

Cyphered dispatch from Mr. . . . Vice-Consul at Ragusa to the Committee at Vienna, dated 26 August, (6 September), 1872.

'After four months' absence, C . . . arrived
' yesterday at Mostar, bringing several letters and
' petitions from the inhabitants of Herzegovina,
' addressed to the Imperial Ministry of Foreign
' Affairs, and to the higher functionaries at St.
' Petersburg.

'Thanks to the zeal and *savoir faire* of C . . .
' the Montenegrin cause has gained ground in that
' country, where even the Catholics begin to be

'accustomed to the idea of one day becoming
'subjects of Prince Nicholas.

'I hope soon to be able to transmit to the
'Committee the interesting and detailed account
'of his journey and of his conversations with the
'monks and the most influential proprietors in the
'country. As to the letters and petitions for St.
'Petersburg I have sent them direct to the Asiatic
'Department.'

'This morning two agents of the Servian
'Society, 'Mlada Srbadia' arrived here. They came
'to see me, and they told me that the chiefs of the
'Society instructed them to visit the convents of
'Herzegovina and Dalmatia, and establish there
'*popular libraries.*'

The "popular libraries" play an important part in the conspiracy, as will appear by the documents further on.

Cyphered dispatch of Mr. . . . Consul at Ragusa, to the Committee at Vienna, 28 August (9 September), 1872.

. . 'Prince Kh . . ., who arrived here the day
'before yesterday, is already at Cettigné. On his
'way he was not only able to see the princely

'family, but to converse with several of our friends
'in this city.

'His arrival at Cattaro having coincided with
'that of V . . . it was easy for me to arrange that
'they should travel together to Montenegro, and
'Mr. Khilkoff writes to me that they intend pro-
'ceeding from thence into Bosnia.

'*I have received the* 10,000 *florins from the*
'*Central Committee, and shall make it my duty to*
'*carry out, as soon as possible, its decision with*
'*regard to the new agency at Budna.* As to the
'aid destined for the Montenegrins I have requested
'M. Kh . . . to remit to Prince Nicholas 3,000
'florins, which his highness will distribute to the
'most necessitous families.'

Here is a consul who "makes it his duty" to
carry out the orders of a secret society, and undertakes to distribute the sums which that society
devotes to the budget of the meditated insurrection.
As to Prince Nicholas he is truly a *grand seigneur*.
He distributes aid to his distressed subjects by
three thousand florins at a time; but it is the same
society which furnishes him the means for this
lavish generosity.

No. 17.

Cyphered dispatch from Mr. . . ., Consul General at Belgrade, to the Committee at Vienna, 1/13 December, 1872.

'I have the honour to announce to the Com-
'mittee at Vienna that, *in conformity with the*
'*instructions of the Central Committee* dated the
'18/30 August, the formation of the Society of
'Liberation is in full progress. M. Ristich having
'accepted the provisional presidency, all the officers
'of the regular army in the principality, and a
'considerable number of those of the National
'Militia, have hastened to inscribe their names on
'the list of members of the Society.

'The day before yesterday and yesterday there
'was such an influx into the offices of the pro-
'visional managers, that we have been obliged to
'open three new agencies:

'1. At the offices of the "Mlada Srbadia."
'2. At the National Casino.
'3. At the house of M. Leschjanin.

'To-day I am sending our J . . . to Seraïevo,
'where he will consult with the Imperial Consul,
'with a view to *beginning our work in Bosnia.*

'Emissaries whom the "Mlada Srbadia" Society
'are sending into Bosnia and Herzegovina:—
  '1. D . . . (priest).
  '2. A . . . (monk).
  '3. D . . . J . . .
  '4. S . . . A . . .
  '5. M . . . F . . .
  '6. M . . . S . . . '

(Translated from Russian.)

The spectacle of a Consul-General who, "in conformity with the instructions of the Central Committee," acts with a view to operations in Bosnia and elsewhere, is truly edifying. That official will, no doubt, feel obliged to us for not having disqualified his acolytes for service in some future contingency by publishing their names at full length.

No. 18.

Cyphered dispatch from the Central Committee to the Committee at Vienna, dated St. Petersburg, 2/14 September, 1872.

'By order of His Imperial Highness Monseig-
'neur, our august President, the Committee at

'Vienna is invited to send two plenipotentiary
'agents to Neusatz, in order to take part in the
'conferences which will be held by the chiefs of
'the national party for choosing candidates to
'stand for the future elections of the Servian
'Patriarch. At the same time you will have to
'send some zealous and intelligent agents into
'Bosnia and Herzegovina, and these will have to
'consult with the emissaries of the "Mlada
'Srbadia" for the formation of popular libraries.
'If the Committee has not at its disposal persons
'capable of fulfilling this task, they can address
'themselves to the Imperial Consuls at Ragusa
'and Seraïevo, and to the Vice-Consul at Mostar,
'who will choose the desired agents. These agents,
'whilst keeping a watch over the proceedings and
'language of the Servian emissaries, will proceed
'to form in the country *a secret society* whose
'members will *bind themselves to fly to arms at the
'first signal*, and to present themselves wherever
'they may be directed to do so by the chiefs of
'the Central Committee.'

(Translated from Russian.)

O! Monseigneur! you who preside in so "august" a manner the Committee in which these conspiracies are centralised, make your mind easy; your "Imperial Consuls" will be well able to find, for a consideration, the devoted champions whom you are in need of. You know that "birds of a feather flock together." Let it be admitted, however, that all these people and things compromise you strangely; and the words "secret society" in a dispatch where you are named, is an awkward fact; for, after all, you are a Highness.

No. 19.

Cyphered dispatch of Mr. . . . Consul at Belgrade to the Committee at Vienna, dated 7/19 September, 1872.

'I hasten to inform you that the Committee at
· Belgrade having entrusted T. . . . P. . . . and
'B. . . . B. . . . with the mission of travelling
'over the *Northern districts of the Vilayet of the*
'*Danube* in order to propagate in those parts the
'ideas of the "Mlada Srbadia" and to establish
'branches of the unionist agency here, those

'gentlemen left Servia on the 4/16 instant for their
'destination.

'T. . . . P. . . . will proceed in the first
'instance to Roustchouk, accompanied by Jovan
'B. . . . and Bogow D. . . .

'B. . . . will stay some days in the neighbour-
'hood of Viddin, where he will be joined by our
'fellow-countryman D. . . . These gentlemen
'having called on me *to take my instructions* before
'their departure, I gave them letters for our
'Consul-General at Roustchouk, as also 250 francs
'to each.

(Translated from Russian.)

No. 20.

Cyphered dispatch of Mr. . . ., Consul at
Seraïevo, to the Committee at Vienna, dated 24
October (5 November) 1872.

'J . . . writes to me from Banja-Luka, under
'date of the 18/30 instant, that he finds himself
'obliged to leave the country for Servia immediately.
'His journey from this to Banja-Luka has been
'effected with great difficulty in consequence of
'the Turkish zabtiehs and soldiers, who have been

'scouring the country in great numbers of late.
'Had he not taken with him our M . . . it would
'have been impossible for him to reach that town
'safe and sound. He was twice even on the point
'of being taken by the Turkish police, who have
'latterly been sent out against the patriotic clergy
'of the country, and he was only able to elude
'them through his presence of mind and his
'friendly relations with the Khodja-bashi.

'Affairs at Banja-Luka are worse than they
'were four months ago. The feverish energy of
'the *Mutesarrif*, which has succeeded his former
'apathy, forms an obstacle which it is impossible at
'present to surmount. In the meanwhile J . . .
'has received new instructions from Kragujewatz
'enjoining him to re-cross the frontier as soon as
'possible, in order to be present at the extraordinary
'assembly of the Srbadia which will take place
'towards the first days of November (N.S.). It is
'M . . . who will remain in his place, and as his
'presence (*especially under the name which he goes
'by here*) cannot excite any suspicion, it is to be
'hoped that the mission confided to J . . . will
'be brought to a successful issue.

'The day before yesterday two Montenegrins arrived here. They have been sent by B ... P ... to come to an understanding with the council of the bishopric as to the number of the pupils whom the diocese of Mgr. Paissios may be sending shortly to the seminary at Cettigné. I greatly doubt whether Mgr. Paissios has the power to do anything in that sense. This worthy prelate has been for some time past in great disfavour with the Turkish authorities, and he will do well (as I have told him) to avoid any step which might cause him to forfeit altogether the confidence of the Turks, and lead to his dismissal when he would doubtless be replaced by some Phanariote, a worthy rival of the ex-metropolitan Dionysius.'

(Translated from Russian).

What a misfortune truly if that gallows-bird J ... had not reached Banja-Luka safe and sound, and if the "worthy" prelate Paissios, assisted by his "patriotic clergy," had had to celebrate masses for his unclean soul! As for the Turkish authorities their effrontery is unparalleled; they are capable of replacing that sainted prelate and conspirator by some " Phanariote " bishop, unworthy enough to feel a respect for the laws.

No. 21.

Cyphered despatch from Mr. . . ., Vice-Consul at Mostar, to the Committee at Vienna, dated 1/13 November, 1872.

'I hasten to acknowledge receipt of the
'packets 418 and 419, which I have forwarded
'immediately to their address.

'Having received at the same time the 750
'ducats destined for the families at Popovo, who
'suffered last year from the Turkish persecutions,
'I communicated with our friend Y . . . with a
'view to his undertaking the distribution of the
'same. As this gentleman cannot proceed to
'those parts at once I have found myself obliged
'to transmit the above sum to the Imperial Con-
'sulate at Ragusa, which has every means of
'getting the money conveyed without impediment
'to its destination.

'I have received a letter from Y . . . an-
'nouncing his arrival at Trebigné. He will only
'remain there a few days, and will be here early

'next week. It seems that his journey has been
'perfectly successful, and that he has no longer
'encountered at Suttorina the obstacles which
'formerly caused so much annoyance to C . . .
'From this place he will proceed, he tells me, to
'Banja-Luka, and perhaps as far as the Austrian
'frontier.'

These packets, Nos. 418 and 419, set us a pondering. As to the 750 ducats, which the Committee sends to the Vice-consul, we are now accustomed to that sort of thing; it is no longer worth while to comment on the fact.

No. 22.

Cyphered dispatch from Mr. . . . Vice-consul at Mostar to the Committee at Vienna, dated 10/22 November, 1872.

'It was only the day before yesterday that I
'received the dispatch of 18/30 October, with the
'proclamation of V . . . I immediately sent for
'our friend J . . . and, after having communicated
'to him your wishes, I gave into his hands a copy
'of the proclamation. The different copies were
'ready by yesterday evening, and to-day our friend

'has been distributing them *among the most in-*
'*fluential of our partizans.*

'As to what concerns the Bishop Procopius,
'I have sent an article against him to Cettigné
'with a letter to B . . . begging him to get it
'published in the *Cesnogorac.*

'After the appearance of this article we shall
'be able to begin with greater effect our pro-
'paganda against that unworthy prelate, and it
'will no longer be difficult to conquer the
'resistance of those whose timidity has so greatly
'hampered us in the accomplishment of our
'wishes.'

The Bishop Procopius has only to take care and sit properly if your article is as well considered as your moral is easy; that "unworthy prelate," after the "propaganda" which will follow your Vice-consular labours as a *litterateur*, may simply be considered as a lost man. What a *worthy* dignitary of the Church he would have been, on the other hand, had he only chanced to be born with some Slavic sentiment in his soul.

No. 23.

Cyphered dispatch from Mr. . . ., Consul at Scutari, to the Committee at Vienna, dated 12/24 November, 1872.

' Our position here is becoming more and more
' intolerable. Notwithstanding the considerable
' number of partizans we have among the moun-
' taineers, and for all that the emissaries of Prince
' Nicholas, who incessantly travel about the country
' in every direction, can do, we find it very difficult
' to struggle against *the intrigues of Shevket.* That
' Turk inspires every one with so great a terror
' that it is impossible to think of creating a diver-
' sion in favour of Montenegro.

' It would be well for the interests of our
' brethren by race, were the Committee to write to
' Constantinople in support of my last report to
' His Excellency the Ambassador. The removal
' of Shevket can alone preserve the country from
' great calamities and fructify our efforts in favour
' of this people, so worthy of our best protection.'

What an *intriguer* is this " Shevket ! " that he dare to give trouble to the promoters of disturbances in the province which he administers ! One must be indeed a Turk to be capable of such conduct. But he will have to deal with the influence of His Excellency, the Ambassador, and he would be a rash man who would give ten para's for Shevket's place.

No. 24.

Cyphered dispatch from the Central Committee at St. Petersburg to Mr. . . . . , Consul at Salonica, under date of Nov. 14/26, 1872.

The Central Committee has the honour to announce to you that, by order of His Imperial Highness our illustrious President, the agency at Mount Athos is to be transferred into an Organizing Committee.

This Committee will have for its mission:—

1. To establish in the convent named " Roussikon " *a depôt of arms and munitions of war:*

2. To send into *Macedonia, Thrace, Bulgaria, and Old Servia emissaries* charged to distribute *books* and *money*, and *to enrol partizans* of the Slavic cause and *volunteers for the patriotic movement.*

3. To establish in the peninsula of Athos Russian and Bulgarian colonies, with a view to

transforming that territory into *an essentially Slavic country*. To this end you will neglect no means to dispossess the Greeks, within the space of some years, of all the convents and lands of Athos which still remain in their possession.

The Organising Committee will have at its disposal annually, *the sum of* 50,000 *roubles*, whose employment *will be controlled by the Imperial Embassy* at Constantinople.

' The direction of the Committee will be confided to the *Imperial Consul* at Salonica who will be bound to reside during half the year at Athos. In his absence the Presidency will pass to the Reverend Father Hieronymus to whom will be adjoined three of the monks whom you have recommended to the protection of the Committee, namely, the Fathers Macarius (of Roussikon), and Benjamin and Stephen (of Lavra).'

His Imperial Highness the August President of the Central Committee began to see things clearly about this time. When the Roussikon should have become a *depôt* of arms, and a centre from which money would be distributed, and where the enrolment of volunteers would be carried on; when the Russian monks should have expelled the Greek monks to an extent which would allow the former to act freely in the neighbourhood, it would then become easy to carry on the work of agitation, and to raise disturbances in the country which might have the effect even of causing the assassination of Consuls—the event, indeed, is there to fill with pride the august personage who has shown himself to have been so far-sighted.

No. 25.

Cyphered dispatch from M . . ., Consul at Scutari, to the Committee at Vienna, 17/29 November, 1872.

'B . . . P . . . has just informed me of the 'return to Cettinyé of the two agents whom he 'sent four months ago into Southern Albania.

'The mission confided to these two emissaries 'was, as you know, to travel over the country 'beyond Dulcigno and to extend the influence of 'Montenegro in those parts. Thanks to the clever-'ness of B . . ., and especially to the pecuniary 'means placed at his disposal by order of the

'Central Committee, this mission has been crowned
'with success.

'Preaching everywhere the holy war against
'the enemies of Slavo-Albanian independence,
'B . . . and his associate *had at the same time to
'speak against the Bulgarians* in order not to arouse
'the somewhat Philhellenic sentiments of the
'Albanians, This line of conduct, *as clever as it
'was wise*, has won over to the Montenegrin
'emissaries *the confidence of the ignorant population
'of the Guegue districts*, and we have grounds for
'hoping that the money so generously expended
'on this occasion will bear good fruit by and bye.

'It is only in the diocese of Janina that B . . .
'failed in his efforts. The influence of the Greek
'Archbishop at that town is so great that our friend
'had to stop short at the first words spoken in the
'sense of his mission. Foreseeing unpleasantness
'and even betrayal, he found it advisable to turn
'back and join his associate who was awaiting him
'for ten days in the neighbourhood of Vallona.

'In communicating to me these details, B . . .
'P . . . added that, according to B . . . the
'influence of R . . . P . . . in the country is so

'insignificant that the inhabitants of several dis-
'tricts in Epirus have lately sent back to Trieste
'the numbers of the *Clio* which took up the
'defence of the Phereistes against the attacks of
'the English party at Corfu.

'M. C . . . seems to be indulging in great
'illusions with regard to the importance and
'the prospects of his task, which will beyond all
'doubt meet with the same fate as the mission
'of our agents at Corfu and in Epirus in
'1870.

'Before working upon the inhabitants of that
'province it would, according to Prince Nicholas
'(and I entirely share his opinion), be necessary to
'contrive that the Archbishop of Janina be re-
'placed by a more ambitious and less philo-Turk
'prelate than the present one. Otherwise, we
'should be turning round in a vicious circle, and
'the more money we disburse the more we shall
'be compromising our cause in those countries.'

This Mr. B . . ., at whose disposal appreciable
"pecuniary means" are placed, and who is so
successful, seems to us to be after all but a very
poor creature. It is instructive to observe how

easily he can bring himself to disavow when circumstances require it, his good friends the Bulgarians. It is to be regretted, at the same time, that this worthy man should have found at Janina so " unambitious " a Bishop as the one who offers so serious an impediment to the progress of the sacred cause. What a " worthy prelate " would this Bishop have been found had he shown himself ambitious to possess himself of some of the " pecuniary means " at the disposal of the excellent Mr. B . . . !

Cyphered dispatch from the Committee at Vienna to Mr. . . . Consul at Seraïevo, 13/25 December, 1872.

'The Committee at Vienna have just sent to
'the Consul-General at Belgrade *the sum of*
'*£. S. 1,400*, with a request to have it conveyed to
'you by the first favourable opportunity. *This*
'*amount has been assigned by the Central Committee*
'*to the orthodox population of Bosnia, with a view*
'*to enabling it to sustain vigorously the struggle*
'against the Phanariote clergy, and *against the*
'*ever-increasing despotism of Turkish rule.* You
'are consequently requested to arrange with

'Monseigneur Paissios and the notables who are
'devoted to our cause as to the best and most
'efficacious employment of the above amount.

'In communicating to you this decision of the
'central committee, we think it necessary to add
'that you are perfectly free to give a part of the
'sum in question to such of the Catholic Monks
'as may possess influence over the Bosniac popula-
'tion. As we have it in view to confirm the ties
'of a good understanding which has latterly
'become established between the principal mem-
'bers of the clergy of the two churches, it would
'give us great happiness were the abbots of the
'catholic convents to support with their influence
'the propaganda of the orthodox clergy for the
'vindication of their rights.

'An identical dispatch has just been sent to
'the Vice-Consul at Mostar, *who will receive*
'*£. S.800, via Ragusa.*'

It is clear that the Turkish Government, which does not make remittances in pounds sterling to be laid out in the purchase of partizans, cannot but be an oppressive government. As to the catholic clergy of Bosnia, whose good understanding with the Russian clergy there is so much anxiety to cement, must we believe that it has not read the history of the Catholic Church in Poland, nor heard of the odious politico-religious pasquinades of Siestrencewitz and Siemasko?

No. 27.

Cyphered dispatch of Mr. . . . Vice-Consul at Mostar, to the Committee at Vienna, dated 14/26 December, 1872.

'Yesterday Mr. B. . . . . B. . . . , the prin-
' cipal agent of the Committee of National Initia-
' tive arrived here. An hour after his arrival he
' presented himself at the Consulate to deliver to
' me a letter from Mr. A. . . . D. . . . , and to
' place himself at my disposal.

'The Secretary of the Committee writes to
' me, that the two Agents sent a couple of months
' ago into Herzegovina, having failed in their
' mission, the Committee has deemed it advisable
' to entrust Mr. G. . . with the same undertaking,
' and to put him in direct communication with
' myself and Mr. C. . . .

'So far as I am able to judge, the choice of
'the Committee has been a more happy one this
'time than last. Mr. G. . . set to work on the very
'day of his arrival here, and we may assure our-
'selves of the success of his mission. As he starts
'to-morrow he leaves in his place at Mostar the
'eldest of the masters of the orthodox school, who
'enjoys a certain degree of consideration in the
'country, and is greatly devoted to us.

'Thanks to the zeal of this last person and to
'the *savoir faire* of Mr. P. . . . ., the bishop
'Procopius was unable to find out anything. I
'believe he is even completely ignorant of the
'arrival of the Servian agent.

'After having travelled over the Eastern parts
'of Herzegovina, T . . . . will proceed to Seraïevo
'which he will reach towards the beginning of
'February. As it is then that the Committee of
'Initiative will be in possession of *the arms for dis-*
'*tribution to the volunteers,* P . . . . . thinks he is
'sure of being able then *to complete the enrolment*
'and to hand over to the new delegates from
'Belgrade *the lists of volunteers* with their
'signatures.'

"Distribution of arms," "enrolment of volunteers,"—such has been the unceasing employment of a certain diplomatist for ten years past. And the cabinet for which this diplomatist was acting is no other than the one which reproaches Turkey with the insurrections thus prepared and fomented by its agents.

Cyphered dispatch of Mr. . . . ., Consul at Tiume, to the Committee at Vienna, 13/25 January, 1873.

'I have just received a letter from Mr. M . . .
'who announces the departure of his secretary for
'Banja-Luka. The object of this journey is *to*
'*establish direct communications between the Orthodox*
'*Clergy of Austrian Servia and that of Bosnia*, with
'the view of the ultimate reunion of those countries
'*under the same ecclesiastical authority.*

'The Montenegrin emissary L . . . arrived
'here four days ago. His journey across Bosnia
'was a real Odyssey, which he will relate to you
'himself soon, for he will be leaving for Vienna in
'eight days. As he was unable to accomplish his
'mission in Bosnia owing to the great vigilance of

'the Turkish police, he has made over the task to
'his friend M . . . of Livno.

'*The pamphlets and the prayer-books* which the
'Committee despatched a month ago reached me
'yesterday. I will send them into Bosnia by the
'first favorable opportunity.'

The methods by which Russia effected a Bulgarian secession from the Greek Church, and her object in so doing, are matter of history. We here recognize the same method and the same object in the project of an union under the same authority of the orthodox clergy of Austria with that of Bosnia. Let the Austrian Government take warning.

No. 29.

Cyphered dispatch from Mr. . . ., Consul at Scutari, to the Committee at Vienna, dated 15/27 January, 1873 :—

'R . . . has sent me a copy of two circular
'letters which *the Albanian refugees in Montenegro*
'have addressed to their fellow-countrymen. The
'writers of these circulars, after setting forth the
'causes which have obliged them to expatriate

'themselves, advise the Albanians to forget their
'internal dissensions and to unite themselves firmly
'with a view to combat the oppressor of their
'country as soon as their valiant allies, the
'Montenegrins, shall enter Albania.

'These circulars, one of which is intended for
'the Servian-Albanians, and the other for the
'inhabitants of the southern districts, are filled
'with expressions of gratitude towards the princely
'Government of Montenegro for the cordial and
'fraternal reception which it has given them and
'their families in the Principality. His Highness,
'according to what R . . . writes me, has ordered
'several thousand copies of these circulars to be
'printed and sent into Albania by special emissaries.

'I learn from Prisrend that the Greco-Walla-
'chians in those parts are agitating strongly to
'get the bishop removed, and that they do not
'hesitate to use any calumny towards that end.
'It is to be hoped, however, that the influence of
'the Imperial Embassy at Constantinople will
'preserve the country from so great a misfortune."

On referring to a preceding dispatch from the
Consul at Mostar (No. 13), the reader will perceive

that these so-called refugees in Montenegro were eighteen agents whom the said Consul had sent there sufficiently provided with funds to be able to promise supplies of gunpowder and arms to those of their accomplices who had to remain behind. The circulars signed by these emissaries have not come into our hands. It would be curious to know whether the writers chose to set forth the *true* motives of their expatriation.

No. 30.

Cyphered dispatch of Mr. . . . , Consul at Seraïevo, to the Committee at Vienna, dated 12/24 January, 1873.

' The news from Prisrend continues satisfactory.
' Thanks to the Patriotism of Mgr M. . . . the
' pretensions of the Koutso-Wallachs have been
' energetically repelled by the members of the com-
' munity, and the Servian cause has triumphed
' over the ambushes laid for it by the Phanariote
' clergy. The arrival of Father A. . . . will, I
' hope, reanimate the courage of our friends, and
' will enable the bishop to struggle with greater
' strength against these new enemies of Slavism.

'As Father A. . . . cannot remain long at Prisrend, he will confide the cypher to the bishop who will henceforward correspond with us direct.

'The distribution of aid in money referred to in my last dispatch took place on the 1/13th instant, at Seraïevo, and on the 6/18th in the neighbouring districts. *As to the arms and munitions*, I have given part of them to B. . . . who has *undertaken to distribute them among our friends at Fravnik*. As regards the remainder I shall await the first favourable opportunity for sending it on *to Prisrend and Detchany*.'

The worthy bishop who does not scruple to correspond in cypher with secret societies and conspirator-consuls, is, we see exposed to the " ambushes of the Phanariote clergy." Side by side with this outburst of virtuous indignation, the distribution of the Committee's arms, gunpowder, and money far and wide in the Turkish provinces, is gravely recorded.

No. 31.

Cyphered dispatch from Mr. . . . Consul at Scutari, to the Committee at Vienna, dated 7/19 February, 1873.

'Radovich writes to me that it was the bad
'weather that prevented the grand review which
'Prince Nicholas intended holding at Tzernoe-
'vitchereka. The review will certainly take place
'nevertheless, for the delegates of the Albanian
'tribes cannot make any long stay in Montenegro
'without exposing themselves to ill treatment on
'the part of the Turkish authorities.

'The Prince reccived, towards the end of last
'month, three priests, of whom, two from Glava
'and Stravisa, belonging to the Orthodox Church,
'and one from Riolli, a Catholic. They came to
'Cettigné *to receive the subsidies* which had been
'promised them by the Prince's government.
'M. Radovich adds that they have promised His
'Highness to conform in all particulars to the
'instructions which were given to them last
'November.

'No sooner was it founded than the fraternity
'at Dulcigno enlarged its circle of action among
'the neighbouring tribes. The Christian popula-
'tion of Alessio seems to be perfectly disposed to
'act in common with that of Dulcigno.'

Here we are again treated to the edifying spectacle of priests—one of them a Roman Catholic—" holding out the hand for Panslavic alms." We use the expressive terms in which, as our readers will remember, the operation is described by the great almoner, Mr. X. . . . himself.

No. 32.

Cyphered dispatch from Mr. . . . Consul at Ragusa, to Mr. Y. . . . at Vienna, dated 16/28 December, 1872.

'Prince Nicholas, having been informed of the
'late decisions of the Central Committee with
'regard to Montenegro, has requested me to convey
'to the Committee the expression of his deep
'gratitude. At the same time he has caused to be
'handed to me an autograph letter for His
'Highness Monseigneur * * which I hasten to
'enclose herewith under flying seal, with the
'request that your Excellency will please to
'forward it to its high destination.

'The letter in question being full of very in-
'teresting and minute details respecting the state
'of the armaments in the principality. I consider

'it useless to trouble your Excellency further on
'that subject. I shall only add that B. . . . has
'lately declared that he can do nothing as regards
'the munitions without the authorisation of Opnich.'

(Translated from Russian.)

Whether Prince Nicholas had real reason thus to testify "his deep gratitude" to the Central Committee, is a question which the future has yet to show. In the meanwhile it is certain that this powerful *officina* of Panslavic insurrection has found it its interest, so far, to draw the petty princeling of Cettigné from the obscurity in which he would otherwise have lived and died, and to make him the tool of its designs.

As to the munitions which are alluded to at the close of this letter, it will be seen further on that they formed part of a large contract passed with the firm of Opnich at Trieste.

No. 33.

Cyphered dispatch from Mr. . . ., Vice-Consul at Mostar, to the Committee at Vienna, 22 December, 1872 (o.s.).

'I have just received a letter from B . . .
'P . . ., who writes at Trebigné the 18/30th
'inst. He has completely succeeded in his mission,
'and *has managed to come to an understanding with*
'*all the chiefs of the districts which he has travelled*
'*through.*

'The Archimandrite M . . ., to whom I had
'recommended P . . ., has greatly assisted him in
'the accomplishment of his task. At the close of
'his letter he announces his departure for Popovo,
'whence he will proceed on the following day to
'Niksich.

'*The chests* 798-801, A.P.C.M. arrived here on
'the 19th instant. I have already *distributed the*
'*contents of* 799 to the persons designated to me,
'and shall not fail to forward the remainder to its
'destination.'

No. 34.

Cyphered dispatch from Mr. . . ., Consul at
Seraïevo, to the Committee at Vienna, 29 December, 1872 (o.s.).

'I learn from Prisrend that the cause of the
'independent church is making sensible progress

'there. The Father A . . . left yesterday for
'Prisrend, and Monseigneur Paissios, and I en-
'trusted him with several letters from Servia for
'the notables of the country, as also with 1,000
'francs for the priests who so courageously defend
'the national cause.

'Mr. B . . . P . . . has written to me lately
'inquiring after his agent L . . . Unfortunately,
'it is not in my power to give any information on
'that head. I learn that that Montenegrin went
'to Banja-Luka some weeks ago and left again
'immediately. That is all I have been able to
'ascertain regarding him, and I am completely
'ignorant as to whether he succeeded or not in
'crossing the Austrian frontier. I have written to
'Agram inquiring about the mysterious disappear-
'ance of this unhappy patriot. It would be a great
'misfortune if he should have fallen into the hands
'of the Turks.

'I have taken the necessary measures for pro-
'ceeding, after the holidays, *to distribute the aid in
'money and munitions of war* which were forwarded
'to me from Belgrade at the beginning of this year,
'and which I *caused to be deposited in the grottoes*

'*which you know.* Having succeeded in *completely lulling suspicion* in this matter, I was enabled last week to get the things in question transported hither, and I trust I shall manage to distribute them without hindrance.'

(Translated from Russian.)

The existence of a depôt of "munitions of war" established by the Consul "in the grottoes which you know," is a fact so impressive in itself when taken with that of the breaking out of the insurrection two or three years later in that neighbourhood, that comment would be superfluous.

No. 35.

Cyphered dispatch from Mr. . . . Consul at Scutari, to the Committee at Vienna, dated 2/13 January, 1873.

'*In conformity with the latest instructions which I have received from the Committee at Moscow,* I have despatched a special messenger to Prisrend, *to convey to the bishop the sum of 500 ducats,* as also the *prayer books* for the Bulgaro-Servian Church.

'The energetic character and the patriotic
'sentiments of this *worthy prelate* lead us to hope
'that the national movement will before long take
'a decisive turn. In order to give an impetus to
'the movement I have written to our agent at
'Detchany to use every endeavour for bringing
'about a reconciliation between the orthodox
'Servians and the Albanians of that district. As
'the two members of the Kiero Committee will be
'in those parts towards the beginning of spring, it
'is to be hoped that they will greatly contribute
'to the success of our plans, the more especially
'since they will be *amply provided with the sinews
'of action.*'

(Translated from Russian.)

It is an understood thing that the "worthy prelate" is invariably the bishop who, in obedience to Russian policy, secedes from the established order of things; whereas the "unworthy prelate" is he who remains faithful to the orthodox Church. But a striking fact is to be noticed: it is always in the category of "worthy prelates" that we find the hand stretched forth to take the vile lucre which pays sold consciences.

The above dispatch, which so justly lays stress on the importance of " the sinews of action " in the work of Panslavic propagandism, will close our second series of documents.

The Consul at Scutari here records that the acts " in conformity with the instructions which he has received from the Committee at Moscow," and that in as unblushing a manner as his colleague at Serajevo just now reported, not without a touch of pride, his success in " lulling suspicion " with regard to the consular *depôts* of munitions of war.

It would offend the moral sense of the reader to comment on such facts as these:—A whole country given up during six years to the dark intrigues of secret societies, whose patrons are princes of Sovereign families, whose accomplices are privileged diplomatists and consuls, and whose agents are dignitaries of the church, giving to their clergy the debasing example of simony.

It is usual to reproach the Porte with these frequent outbreaks in his provinces which, like volcanic eruptions, threaten destruction over an area which no foresight can measure. In real conscience we believe that, after a perusal of the foregoing pages, but one sentiment can find a place in the mind of the reader,—that of surprise that the Empire which it is a conventional commonplace to represent as spontaneously falling to pieces, has had enough vitality to resist until now the powerful dissolvents which have been applied to its body politic with arts so insidious and satanic.

VI.

We have let ourselves into the most intimate confidence of the big-wigs of Russian diplomacy, and we know the principles by which they are guided; we have seen to what a formidable conspiracy they lent the support of their high position. We have next followed the details of the operations of their subordinates, whereby the plot was prepared to be put into execution.

To complete the brief it will be sufficient to place under the eyes of the reader, by way of specimen, some of the instructions and deliberations of the insurrectional committees, by whose tenour chiefs and subalterns were alike inspired.

No. 36.

Cyphered despatch from the Central Committee to the Committee at Vienna, dated St. Petersburg, 9/21 August, 1872.

'By order of His Imperial Highness Mon-
'seigneur * * *, the Vienna Committee is enjoined
'to send all the sub-committees and agencies a
'circular dispatch to tranquilise our brethren by
'race with regard to the false reports which our
'enemies are endeavouring to propagate among the
'Slavs concerning the interview of the three
'emperors at Berlin.

'Sincerely devoted as it is to the Slavic cause,
'and ever interested in the prosperity and the
'future of our brethren by race, the Imperial
'Government in no wise entertains the idea which
'is attributed to it by those secular enemies of
'Slavism, the Poles, to abandon the Slavs to their
'fate, and to bind themselves by a solemn treaty
'with Germany and Austria.

'Whilst desirous of peace and of the consoli-
'dation of public order in Europe, Russia will
'never allow herself to deviate from the line of
'conduct which she has so gloriously inaugurated

'since the accession to the throne of His Majesty 'the Emperor Alexander II.

'You will write then to your agents desiring 'them to communicate to all our friends the tenour 'of the present dispatch, at the same time assuring 'them that, notwithstanding her profound desire 'for peace, Russia will never leave her brethren by 'race without aid and assistance, and that she 'remains, as in the past, ready for every sacrifice in 'order to ensure them a future worthy of the race 'to which we have, all of us, the happiness to belong.'

The " public order " whose " consolidation in Europe " is desired by Russia is—let us not forget it—that order without equilibrium which enables her to work without danger, even were it by those means which may threaten the repose of that same Europe, to ensure to the Slavs " a future worthy of the race " to which the " august President " of the Central Committee has " the happiness to belong."

No. 37.

Cyphered dispatch from the Central Committee to the Committee at Vienna, dated 17/29 August, 1872.

'By order of His Highness Monseigneur * *
'you are enjoined to establish, as soon as possible,
'a special agency at Viddin. Its functions being
'already defined by the circular of the Central
'Committee, dated the 25th July, 1871, § 3; the
'Committee has only to add that by order of our
'Illustrious President an extraordinary credit is
'opened in your favour for 5,000 roubles, for the
'expenses of instalment and maintenance of that
'agency up to the 1st January, 1873.'

(Translated from Russian.)

Viddin is one of the strongholds of the Turkish quadrilateral. The solicitude of the Central Committee and of its "illustrious President" must necessarily be extended to it. To endow Viddin with a "special agency," even at the cost of 5,000 roubles per quarter, was obviously a first-class necessity.

No. 38.

Extract from the Minutes of the sitting of the Moscow Committee of 26 September (8 October), 1872.

'The sitting was opened by Monsieur P . . .
'who read out a pamphlet lately published con-
'taining the biography of A. H . . . Mr. A . . .
'having proposed to commemorate the striking
'services rendered by the illustrious deceased to the
'Slavic cause and Sclavic science, Prince B . . .
'A . . . Tch . . ., and the Secretary of the
'Committee N . . . P . . . submitted to the
'approval of the Committee the following pro-
'positions:—

'1. To found a bursary at the Slavic school
'of the nunnery of Alexeyevsk for a young lady
'*of Bulgarian nationality*, this foundation to be
'called "the Bursary of A. H . . .

'2. To open a subscription among the members
'of the Sclavic Committees and Sub-committees
'towards a capital to be applied to the foundation
'of a prize for the best works on Servia.

'3. To publish, at the expense of the Com-
'mittee, all the unpublished writings of A. H . . .

'These proposals were carried unanimously.

'The Secretary, N. A. P . . ., communicated
'to the members of the Committee the names of
'Slavic pupils newly arrived in Russia, and

'admitted to the Crown schools since the last
'sitting (of 22 July, o.s.)

'After a speech by N. A . . ., on the urgent
'necessity of a moral union among all Slavs in
'order to combat the enemies of Slavism, Mr.
'P . . . brought the sitting to a close by inviting
'the effective members of the political section of
'the Committee to pass into the chamber of
'secret sittings.

'SECRET SITTING.

'The sitting was opened by N. A. P . . ., who
'read out the statement of receipts and expen-
'diture for the 2nd quarter of 1872.

'RECEIPTS.

		ROUBLES.
'1°.	Government subsidy	66,666$\frac{2}{3}$
'2°.	Amount of various gifts	2,874
'3°.	Interest (at 5 per cent.) of the capital of 50,000 roubles, bequeathed by Count Gregory C . . . B	2,500·
'4°.	Interest of the amounts bequeathed by G . . . P . . ., &c., forming together the sum of 18,400 roubles...................................	920·
	Total	72,960·$\frac{2}{3}$

'EXPENDITURE.

		ROUBLES.
'1°.	Maintenance of 216 bursers of the Committee at the Universities and Special Schools, at the rate of 25 roubles per month each	21,600·
'2°.	Ordinary expenses for the permanent agents in the Sclavic provinces of *Austria* and Turkey (65 persons)	13,000·
'3°.	Extraordinary expenses for emissaries in *Bulgaria*, *Gallicia*, *Bohemia*, and *Hungarian Russia*	2,500·
'4°.	Cost and expenses of conveying books and church furniture for reading rooms, churches, and convents in Turkey and *Austria*	1,330·
'5°.	Secret expenses of the President, in conformity with § 12 of the statutes	1,680·
	'Total	40,110·

'The surplus of 32,850·¾ roubles has served to cover 'almost entirely the deficit of the preceding quarter (34,760·¼ 'roubles). The remainder of the deficit (1,909·¾ roubles) will 'be covered in the course of the present quarter.

'The same Mr. N. A. P . . . then presented to the mem- 'bers of the Committee the photographic portrait of the 'Bulgarian Exarch. Anthimos. This portrait has been sent by 'His Holiness to the Moscow Committee with his apostolic 'benediction.

'It was thereupon unanimously decided to have a consider- 'able number of copies of the portrait taken for distribution among 'all the friends of the holy Bulgarian cause. As to the original 'portrait, it will be placed among those of the illustrious men

'of Slavia. Upon the proposal of Prince T . . ., the Com-
'mittee decided to address to the Exarch. through the medium
'of the Imperial Embassy at Constantinople, a letter of thanks
'and of assurances of the fraternal sentiments of the Russian
'people towards all the Slavs of Turkey, and especially towards
'the Bulgarians who hold firmly aloft the Slavic flag against
'the intrigues of the Phanariotes.'

The above budget, which, for one amongst the numerous committees established in Russia, Austria, Turkey and perhaps elsewhere, shows a revenue of more than 72,000 roubles a quarter (about £.S. 50,000 a year), affords an idea of the sacrifices which Panslavism is making to attain its ends. In the face of this fact, one asks one's self how Turkey, a poor country, unversed in modern political practices, has held her own against efforts so prodigious.

These general reflections are of more weight than the details of the budget, valuable as are the lessons which those details teach us. At the same time other cabinets than those of the Sultan have cause to be edified by the latter. We find, under the head of "Expenses," items numbered 2, 3 and 4, which serve to show that the Chancellor of Austro-Hungary was not aware whither he was conducting the affairs of his sovereign and his country when he made himself a complaisant arbitrator in the political suit brought on by the interesting clients of the " ordinary " secret agents which the Moscow Committee of Insurrection, for one, employs in Austria, without reckoning the " extraordinary " agents with which that Committee and all the others favour the Austro-Hungarian Empire.

Notwithstanding the length of the above minute we have considered it essential to reproduce it *in extenso*. It comprises details which, it is true, are of no great interest, but it is the *ensemble* which is instructive; in that it gives an idea of the regular and orderly procedure of assemblies of this kind—of the method whereby ordinary sittings pass into secret ones, and of all the resources and powerful springs of action possessed by these dangerous associations, which an essentially conservative and monarchial Government does not hesitate to protect and encourage with a view to satisfy its ambitious projects.

No. 39.

Cyphered dispatch from Mr. . . ., member of the Central Committee, to the Committee at Vienna, dated 20 October (2 November) 1872.

'By order of His Imperial Highness, Mon-
' seigneur our August President, the Committee at
' Vienna is desired to send two trustworthy men
' to Scutari and Banja-Luka. The person who
' proceeds to Scutari will have the mission of
' arranging with the Imperial Consul as to the
' safest means of reaching the Mirdites.

'The emissary in question must therefore be
' thoroughly acquainted with the country and the
' language of the Albanians. His mission will
' consist in the first place *in the distribution of relief*
' *to the members of the families which have
' suffered from the late measures of repression on the
' part of the Turkish authorities*, and in the
' endeavour to raise the courage of the population
' by means of *various presents* and assurances of a
' speedy and efficacious *intervention of the European
' Powers in their favour.* Our Consul at Scutari
' will point out to your agency the Catholic Monks
' and Priests who have been gained over to the

'Slavic cause, as also such of the chiefs as are
'undoubtably favourable to the Slavic cause. After
'the accomplishment of his mission, your agent
'will await at Scutari the arrival of Mr. P. . . .
'who will be there by the beginning of March to
'complete *our topographical surveys.*

'As to the person who will have to proceed to
'Banja-Luka, it would in our opinion be preferable
'to select him from among the subordinate mem-
'bers of the sub-committee at Belgrade. You
'will thereupon write to Mr. B. . . . and will remit
'him 1,500 florins which you will pass in account
'under the head of extraordinary expenses, § 2.
'The agent in question will have to come to an
'arrangement with the clergy of those parts for the
'establishment of a primary school. The books
'necessary for this purpose will shortly be sent by
'the Central Committee.

'After having travelled through the country
'and worked in favour of *ecclesiastical autonomy*,
'this agent will have to proceed to Seraïevo and to
'await there the ulterior instructions of the Consul-
'General at Belgrade.'

(Translated from Russian.)

To "distribute relief to the members of the families which have suffered from the late measures of repression by the Turkish authorities" was in truth a good means of "raising the courage," that is to say, of encouraging them not to cease the disorders which called for that "repression."

The Slav clergy, the Catholic Monks, every element of moral influence was combined to act upon the minds of the ignorant population, which was to be endowed with "schools" where were to be instilled the principles of revolt, and the Consular authorities were to support with their *prestige* these sagaciously combined plans, contributing at the same time the fruits of their experience as to the men most deeply imbued with the spirit of insurrection. Any means, moreover, were considered legitimate to attain this end, the most unblushing falsehoods not excepted. The "promises of intervention by the European powers" were certainly well calculated to produce a great effect on those poor peasants, too ignorant to be capable of appreciating the stark falsehood of such allegations. Lastly, let us point out the significance of the term "ecclesiastical autonomy" which occurs in this dispatch. Does it not reveal the same fertility of resource in the work of disintegration as that which has since invented the kindred device of *administrative autonomy?*

No. 40.

Cyphered dispatch from the Committee at Vienna to the Central Committee, dated 7/19 November, 1872.

'The Committee at Vienna has the honour to
'inform you that the instructions contained in the
'dispatch of His Excellency Mr. K. . . . dated
'St. Petersburg, 20 October, (2 November) are
'already in full course of execution. Mr. A. . . .
'whom the Committee has chosen for the mission
'to Scutari, left Vienna the 4/16 instant, bearing a
'letter of recommendation to the Imperial Consul
'at Scutari, to whom he will moreover have to
'communicate a copy of the above-mentioned
'dispatch from Mr. K. . . .

'Having telegraphed to Belgrade on the subject
'of the Banja-Luka affair the Committee has been
'informed in reply that it is young D. . . . who
'will have to undertake the journey in question.

'We consequently remitted the day before yesterday to the Consulate-General at Belgrade 1,500 florins, which are entered in account under the head of extraordinary expenses § 2, in conformity with the instructions of the Central Committee.'

(Translated from Russian.)

The writer of the previous dispatch is an Excellency; the above, in reply to it, acquaints us with the fact when it states that the instructions of the said Excellency have been promptly attended to. Nothing can exceed the business-like regularity with which these irregular transactions are conducted.

No. 14.

Deliberations of the Central Committee. The Central Committee, on the 11/23 December, 1872, passed a very important resolution.

'The Slavic Committees established in Russia and their branches abroad have been founded with the view of protecting Slavic interests and of facilitating our brethren in the accomplishment of

'their duties towards the entire race. Considering
'that those of our brethren who emigrate from their
'native countries in order to settle in Russia, in-
'stead of serving the interests of Slavism, do but
'serve those of *Germanism* and *Magyarism* in
'Austria, and of *Islamism* and *Hellenism* in
'Turkey, the Central Committee, in accord with
'the political section, decrees:

'1. That all the Committees in Russia, as also
'the Sub-Committees and Agencies abroad be en-
'joined to cease from the 1st January, 1873, giving
'aid and assistance to the Slavs in Austria and in
'Turkey who may wish to come into Russia in
'order to settle there.

'2. That the Committees, Sub-Committees and
'Agencies be enjoined to announce to our brethren
'by race that the Slavic countries under the foreign
'yoke, having need of the co-operation of all their
'children to struggle against the traditional enemies
'of the Slavic cause, those who should quit their
'native country would lose the right to relief from
'the Russian Committees.

'3. That only those persons who may be com-
'promised towards the political authorities of their

'countries will have the right to apply to the Slavic
'Committees for the means to enable them to pass
'into Russia.

'4. That all the sums hitherto set apart to
'facilitate the immigration of Slavs into Russia
'will be divided among the sub-committees and
'agencies abroad, in order to be distributed among
'those of our brethren who will render most service
'to the Slavic cause.'

(Translated from Russian.)

Without these resolutions of the Central Committee we might possibly have witnessed a general depopulation of the Slavic provinces of Turkey and Austria, and thus the Slavic question in the East will have ceased to exist.

No. 42.

Cyphered dispatch from Mr. . . ., Secretary to the Committee at Moscow to the Committee at Vienna, dated Moscow, 26 December, 1872 (o.s.).

'The Moscow Committee having decided, at
'its secret sitting of the 24 December (5 January),
'to *stimulate the ecclesiastical propaganda in Bosnia
'and Herzegovina, the sum of* 2,500 *roubles* has

'been allotted to that object. In communicating
'this decision to the Committee at Vienna,—I have
'to add that our president requests you to transmit
'the above sum to Mostar and Seraïevo imme-
'diately, and to *require the Imperial Consul* residing
'at those places to furnish you with minute details
'of the manner in which this project of our
'Committee is carried out.'

(Translated from Russian.)

Here then we have the secret committees of Panslavism "requiring" the "Imperial Consuls" to give them a minute account of the employment of their time and of the funds entrusted to them for the purpose of promoting religious dissensions.

No. 43.

Cyphered dispatch from the Central Committee to the Committee at Vienna, dated St. Petersburg, 27 December, 1872 (o.s.).

'The Vienna Committee is requested to inform
'the chief agency at Belgrade that, owing to the
'Turkish government having sent a commission of
'enquiry to Bulgaria, it will be prudent to suspend
'for a while the despatch of emissaries into the

'districts of Routschouk and Viddin. All that
'the chief agency at Belgrade can do just now will
'be to keep up active relations with Toultcha and
'the Dobrudja. The opportunity of exercising
'this activity is *the more favourable since the
'Turkish authorities no longer pay any attention to
'what is going on at Toultcha.* We have taken
'advantage of this by sending the Staff-Captain
'A . . . P . . . to those parts.

'Be so good as to write to Scutari that the
'Imperial Government is ready to admit to the
'Military Schools two Albanian children, who will
'have to proceed to Kiew provided with Monte-
'negrin passports.'

(Translated from Russian.)

The " Staff-Captain A . . . P . . . " will no doubt feel obliged to us for confining ourselves to the initials of his name. Not but that it is sometimes an honour for an officer to have introduced himself secretly into a fortified place in time of war, and for purposes of war. In such cases the danger incurred excuses the nature of the act committed; craft then is devotion, and devotion is courage. But in times of peace, and at the bidding of a secret society, an occupation of that sort is one from which the epaulettes of an officer can hardly come out clean.

No. 44.

Cyphered dispatch from Mr. . . . . member of the Central Committee to the Committee at Vienna, dated St. Petersburg, 31 January, (12 February) 1873.

'By order of His Highness Monseigneur * * the Vienna Committee is enjoined to send im-
' mediately one of its members to Kragujevatz to
' preside over the meeting of the chief clubs of the
' National Initiative. This delegate will be careful
' to direct the action of the clubs towards the end
' which we pointed out in our telegram dated the
' 18/30 October, 1872. He must consequently
' require of the "Mlada Srbadia" that *the arms*
' which they may have received from the Servian
' Government as well as those from our agency, be
' dispatched without loss of time *towards the*
' *Turkish frontier.*

' Our diplomatic agency at Belgrade will receive
' the necessary instructions for facilitating the

'accomplishment of the mission of your delegate, 'and placing at his disposal the sums of money of 'which he may have need.

'After terminating his task at Kragujevatz 'your delegate will have to proceed to Bucharest in 'order to arrange with the chiefs of the Bulgarian 'Committee as to the basis upon which the *new* '*national clubs* are to be established *in the towns* '*and large villages on the right bank of the Danube.*'

'*N.B.*—It is D. . . ., member of the Com-'mittee at Vienna and sub-chief of the Agency at 'Pesth, who has been entrusted with this mission. He leaves Pesth on the 5/17 February.'

(Translated from Russian.)

The plot thickens with the opening of a new year. "National clubs"—in other words, sub-committees of insurrection—are being organized in Bulgaria. The "Mlada Srbadia," a young Servian society is roundly ordered to despatch the arms which it has received *from the Servian Government*, as well as those contributed from Russia to the Turkish frontier. We learn at the same time that a Panslavic agency exists at the capital of Hungary; and it is from that focus of

Slavophobism that the delegate charged with the accomplishment of the above objects has been despatched.

No. 45.

Cyphered dispatch from the Agency at Belgrade to the Committee at Vienna, dated 6/18 February, 1873.

'*The arms which the august members of the 'Imperial Family were pleased to send into Servia*, 'have already reached Belgrade. Thanks to the 'zeal and clever management of Mr. G . . ., the 'conveyance of these was effected with the greatest 'promptitude, and *without awakening the slightest 'suspicion on the part of the riverain authorities.*

' Monsieur Ristich informed us yesterday that 'it has been decided to send new emissaries to 'Prisrend and as far as Okhrida to give an im-'petus to the ecclesiastical movement, which has 'slackened there owing to the late intrigues of the 'Phanar. It would be desirable for Y . . . and 'H . . . to advise Prince Nicholas to despatch 'thither, on his part, some agents to work at the 'realisation of this Slavic object.'

(Translated from Russian.)

For the "august members" of an "Imperial family" to send, in a time of profound peace, "arms" which have to be conveyed "without awakening the slightest suspicion on the part of the riverain authorities," is a very clever proceeding, perhaps, but certainly far from being a correct one.

No. 46.

Cyphered dispatch from Mr. . . ., member of the Central Committee to the Committee at Vienna, dated St. Petersburg, 10/22 February, 1873.

'Send immediately to H . . . 15,000 florins
'for the Belopavlitchy ammunition, Opnich's con-
'tract. The President of the Committee *approves*
'the request of the Christians of Popovo and
'Trebigné; do you then arrange with the *Embassy*
'and Y . . . to *furnish promptly to the population*
'*the arms and ammunition* which it needs.

'*N.B.*—Mr. H . . . is Consul at Trieste, where
'is also the firm of Opnich, which has contracted
'to supply ammunition to the Montenegrin tribe,
'Belopavlitchy.'

(Translated from Russian.)

No. 47.

Cyphered dispatch from Mr. . . ., Delegate of the Vienna Committee to the Committee at Vienna, dated Kragujevatz, 15/27 February, 1873.

'The chiefs of the National Initiative Clubs,
' whom I assembled this morning, have informed
' me that their agents are already installed in the
' principal spots in Old Servia. The accounts
' which they receive pretty regularly from them
' are very encouraging, with the exception of those
' from the Southern parts of the province.

' After having explained to these gentlemen
' the views of the Committee and the instructions
' which you have desired me to communicate to
' them, they placed themselves entirely at my dis-
' posal. Two of these gentlemen (Y . . . B . . .
' and M . . . D . . .) being likewise leading
' members of the " Mlada Srbadia," they assured
' me that their Society is ready to forward towards
' the Turkish frontier the arms which it received
' some time ago.

' The Servian Government, whilst affecting
' ignorance of what is going on at Kragujevatz, is
' none the less very well disposed towards the

'Initiative Clubs. Four days ago Lieut.-Colonel
'Leschjanin (a secret member of the "Mlada
'Srbadia") conveyed to our friends 1,000 ducats
'from the Prince.

'I start the day after to-morrow for Bucharest,
'whence I will write to you on arrival.

'Names of the agents whom the Servian Com-
'mittee of National Initiative has lately sent into
'Old Servia:—
 '1. S . . . B . . .
 '2. M . . . V . . .
 '3. T . . . M . . .
 '4. Y . . . G . . .
 '5. N . . . T . . .
 '6. B . . . C . . .'

(Translated from Russian.)

Instead of limiting ourselves to their initials, we ought perhaps to have given at full length the names of these six agents; but our object is not to inflict the stigma of publicity upon persons; it is the higher and more comprehensive one of bringing to light, in the public interests of Europe, the vast conspiracy which has led to the present state of affairs in the north-west provinces of

Turkey, and which now threatens the repose of the whole civilised world. Here is a wide-spreading net work of secret societies, richly endowed and powerfully supported, which covers a large part of two European empires, and through whose means Russia, by setting the match to the well-laid train, can produce an explosion at any point and at any moment which may suit her selfish and ambitious purposes.

VII.

In the preceding pages we have been enabled to study the aspect of conspirators of low degree, the method of diplomatic agents of middle rank, and the style of ambassadors and other excellencies. Let us now observe the tone of highnesses.

No. 48.

Letter from His Highness Monseigneur * * * * to His Imperial Highness Monseigneur *, dated Cettigné, 10/22 December, 1872.

'The sentiments of high benevolence and of 'lively interest which your Imperial Highness 'unceasingly evinces towards my valiant but

'unfortunate people, encourage me to address
'your Imperial Highness and to expose to you
'truthfully the sad position in which we find our-
'selves, and the almost superhuman efforts to which
'my government is obliged to have recourse, in
'order not to be taken at unawares.

'By the two letters which I have ventured to
'address your Imperial Highness in the months of
'September and October, your Imperial High-
'ness will have seen what the affair of Kolashin
'and the abandonment in which we have found
'ourselves have cost us, thanks to the exigencies of
'a policy opposed to any Slavic movement. Since
'the day when the valiant defenders of the last
'asylum of the liberties of the South Slavs thought
'it their duty to throw themselves against the bar-
'barian enemies of our religion, we find ourselves
'hemmed in with a girdle of iron, which is ever
'pressing more closely upon us and will un-
'fortunately end by provoking conflicts far more
'sanguinary than that of Kolashin.

'The reports of M. J . . . having duly apprised
'the Imperial Ministry of *all the intrigues and*
'*machinations of the Turkish authorities in Albania,*

'I deem it useless to revert to that subject,
'and shall confine myself to adding this much,
'that, thanks to the resources both in money and
'in arms which are at the disposal of my neigh-
'bours at Scutari, my allies of yesterday for the
'most part now hold aloof from us; we shall in all
'probability end by losing the rest, unless the
'Imperial Government comes to our assistance at
'this critical moment.

'In order to counteract the *mines and ambushes*
'which have been prepared for us towards Albania,
'I have sent numerous agents into the frontier
'districts. *My emissaries* have even succeeded in
'reaching the most distant points of Albania and
'in obtaining some successes there. But your
'Imperial Highness will easily understand that
'those successes by no means guarantee the future
'to us, owing to the paucity of our means and the
'numerous detachments of troops which hold the
'shores of the lake of Scutari.

'What consoles us a little in the sad position
'in which we find ourselves is the development
'which the establishment at Tchernævitz-Retchka
'is taking every day. Thanks to the zeal of

'Messieurs S . . . and B . . . we have already
' collected 12,000 Krenk muskets, 4,500 Berdous,
' 6,800 American pistols, 7,000 dragoon sabres and
' 3 mountain batteries. *When we shall have re-*
' *ceived the mitrailleuses and mortars, together with*
' *the* 25,000 *American carbines and the cartouches*
' *and munitions of war which the Imperial Govern-*
' *ment had promised us, we shall be in a position to*
' *begin the struggle.* In the meanwhile I get some
' hundreds of young men from the interior *and*
' *from the frontier provinces* to come every month to
' Retchka and to Negosh and be there exercised
' in the use of European arms. Thanks to this
' system, which is adapted to the manners of the
' country, we shall be in a position to throw out in
' case of need *more than* 30,000 *men perfectly drilled*
' *and burning with the desire to fight the common*
' *enemy.*

'The only thing which troubles us is *the*
' *armaments and fortifications of the Turks, which*
' *we are prevented from putting a stop to.* It is
' upon this very point that I take the liberty to
' draw the attention of your Imperial Highness.

'The counsels which we receive from the
'Imperial Government would be very useful for
'the *development* of my country, *if only the Turks
'would keep quiet.* Unhappily, such is not the
'case. Whilst we are obliged to remain with our
'arms crossed *our neighbours are fortifying them-
'selves and taking the necessary measures to cut us
'off from all access to the interior of Albania and
'Herzegovina.* If this state of things endures for
'another ten months or so we shall find ourselves
'in the absolute impossibility of undertaking
'anything serious against the Turks, whereas the
'latter will be able to penetrate with ease into our
'territory and to repeat there the slaughter of the
'last campaign.

'In submitting these considerations to the high
'appreciation of your Imperial Highness, I venture
'to solicit your intercession in our favour with the
'Imperial Government. My people, Monseigneur,
'rests its whole hope on the magnanimous heart
'*of the Great Emperor of Russia the All Powerful
'Father* and protector of the Slavic family. Your
'Imperial Highness who have so often manifested
'your benevolent solicitude towards my people, will,

'I venture to hope, deign to crown your benefits, *by* '*obtaining for us in the first place a new supply of* '*arms and munition of war, and next,* authorisation 'to march against the enemy of our holy religion 'and of the Slavic race. It is in this hope that I 'have the honour to be, &c.'

This letter is, beyond dispute, a master-piece of its kind. Whilst craft contends with humility, ambition here stands confessed in all its naked simplicity. The writer is making, he says, "almost superhuman efforts;" but when he explains that he is " obliged " to do so " in order not to be taken at unawares," we are irresistibly reminded of the case of " The Wolf and the Lamb," and the moral of that fable suggests itself more and more forcibly as we read on. His Highness complains of the " intrigues and machinations of the Turkish authorities in Albania " whose effect is to " cut us off from all access to the interior of Albania and Herzegovina," and of the " mines and ambushes " prepared against them in that quarter; and, in the same breath reports that he is inundating those same countries with his emissaries, and not without success. The cool and apparently unconscious cynicism of the complaint and the avowal really takes away one's breath. But this is not all. After having complacently detailed the formidable war-material which he has amassed in his arsenal of Tchernœvitz-Retchka; after recapitulating, in a sort of loving spirit, the "muskets" the "pistols," the "sabres," and the "mountain batteries," already in store; after computing, in a tone of desire, the "mitrailleuses," the "mortars," the "carbines," the "cartouches," and the "other munitions of war," which are to be added to the stock, for the "Imperial Government"—not, however, the *Imperial Government* of his suzerain—has "promised" them to him; after explaining that he entices the young men of the "frontier provinces" into his Principality to be there drilled with a view to taking part in the attack which he is meditating against the Turks; after all these candid statements, the Prince dolefully sets forth the defensive measures so maliciously and provokingly taken by the Porte, and which threaten to mar the success of his little plans and preparations; he is "troubled" by the "armaments and fortifications of the Turks," and expresses a proper sense of injury at being "*prevented from putting a stop to them!*"

But it is necessary to repress the sense of the ridiculous which is provoked by this staggering logic, for we must not forget that the subject is a serious one. Let us, then, in all seriousness address His Highness some remarks.

You, Prince, have acquired a certain title to respect; for if the policy you have adopted has been a false one, you have at least given proofs, it is said, of true bravery. And something tells us that your enemies of to-day will perhaps be your best friends to-morrow. Let us then say it, Prince, with the sincere deference which is due to your high rank, "the enemy of your holy religion" is not the Turk, who has always left you free—you and yours—to practise it in your own way; it is he who has sown in your Church the seeds of discord, as a consequence of which you have had for ministers of religion ministers to ambitious projects, whose first intended victim is perhaps yourself. Let your Highness believe this. The enemy of the race to which you belong is not the Turk, who is now inaugurating an era of liberty, in order to make it forgotten that there was once an era of conquest; no, your enemy, Prince, the enemy of your race, is he who only styles himself "the all-powerful father and protector of the Slavic family" in order one day to subject, enslave and annihilate its remaining members, as he has been endeavouring for the last century to do with the noble race of the Jagellons, among whom he came in like manner as a protector and a father. Seek, Prince, in the past the key to the secrets of the future. It is time to do so.

We have said that the conspiracy did not confine its field of operations to the European provinces of Turkey alone; that it likewise extended to those of Asia and Africa. We should fear to tire the attention of the reader by engrafting on the Slavic question others which will find a place elsewhere. We shall, therefore, confine ourselves to the reproduction of the following document:—

Confidential letter from Mr. X . . . to His Highness Monseigneur * * * * * dated Pera, Constantinople, 18/30 May, 1871.

'I hasten to thank Your Highness for the letter with which you have been pleased to honour me, dated Cairo, the 8th instant.

'I believe I ought at the same time to inform you, Monseigneur, that the Imperial Consul-General in Egypt has given me an account of the interview with which Your Highness has honoured him.

"I am very sorry that Your Highness should have attributed to the news which I conveyed to you by my letter of the 15th April, quite a different meaning to that which I had in view. If Your Highness will be pleased to call to mind what I said when I communicated the information in question, you will find that I congratulated Your Highness on the favourable turn which affairs in the East are beginning to take. I remarked that Europe is so exhausted by the last war, and the public mind so desirous of peace that the first who might wish to disturb it would at once be placed under the ban of European Society. What then could be more fortunate for your Highness, than if Turkey, spurred on from all sides were madly to throw herself against Egypt, without a

'legitimate and real cause? The Government of
'Your Highness would only have to defend itself
'for some days, protesting at the same time against
'the spirit of Ottoman conquest, and intervention
'would make head against all obstacles and be
'called for even by those who persist in representing
'us as the missionaries of revolution in the East.

'Whilst reminding you, Monseigneur, of these
'considerations I will permit myself to explain yet
'more clearly the way of thinking of the Imperial
'Government. For the success of our projects it
'is urgent that Egypt should yet remain quiet.
'Arm yourself, make all the preparations necessary
'for a long war, enter into offensive and defensive
'treaties with Greece, Servia, and Roumania (in
'which we will undoubtedly assist you), and con-
'tinue to dispute inch by inch the pretensions of
'the Suzerain Court. Let the Egyptian Govern-
'ment show itself dignified and inflexible in its
'relations with the Porte and it can make sure of
'being victorious. The more firm and intractable
'they find you the more the irritation of the
'Sultan's Ministers will increase, and it will end in
'an explosion. It is then that Egypt will know

'and appreciate Russian friendship, so very different
'from the French protection, which, after urging
'the illustrious grandfather of Your Highness to
'war, was content to lend her a platonic support,
'and to abandon her to Ottoman vengeance.

'I have the honour to be,' &c.

It is necessary to state that the letter of 8th May, to which the above is a reply, expressed lively apprehensions with regard to the "coercive measures" which the "Ministry of Aali Pasha" seemed disposed to have recourse to. Mr. X . . ., as will be seen, reassures his illustrious correspondent as to the consequences which those measures might entail. "Arm yourself," he says, "make all the preparations necessary for a long war, enter into offensive and defensive treaties with Greece, Servia, and Roumania." When an "explosion" has been brought about, then you will know the value of "Russian friendship." Coercive measures, then, far from offering any motive for fear, were, on the contrary, to be courted. That is to say, it was necessary to bring about the "explosion," even though the credulous person who might trust to these fine promises were the first whom it would send flying. Happily for himself, he to whom these insidious counsels were addressed had the wisdom to step back from the precipice down which he was being decoyed.

VIII.

We shall go no further. The above document will be the last of the series. It has a real value, not only because it shows that the conspiracy reached the furthest limits of the Empire, but also as giving an idea of the seductive methods employed by the wily Mr. X. . . . "Get yourself thrashed, so that " we may have an opportunity of coming to your aid, and thus enabling you to enjoy the advantage of our *friendship*." Although this pitiful logic failed to deceive the Prince to whom it was addressed, another Highness was less wise, and unhappy Servia knows what has been the consequence. So do likewise the thousands of ignorant peasants whom it is more easy to excuse for having been dazzled by the prospective of felicity opened up to them through the friendship of the "all-powerful protector and father of the Slavic family."

IX.

Conclusion.

We had promised to strike the BALANCE OF RESPONSIBILITIES. Our end is now obtained. A perusal of the documents which fill this little work can leave no room for further doubt: the Eastern crisis is the result of a Foreign Conspiracy.

There is no limit to the effrontery of the Conspirator. Having provoked the revolt, he now raises obstacles against the work of pacification. He requires that the execution of the reforms shall be guaranteed. Guaranteed by whom? By himself! Let us see how he performs his own promises; then alone may we judge how far he may be trusted to guarantee the promises of others.

At the time of the Congress at Paris, Europe, moved at the sufferings of Poland, wished to raise the question of that unhappy country. Count Orloff, the Russian Plenipotentiary, intimated that the Emperor Alexander desired to inaugurate his reign by measures of liberation which should embrace in their scope all his Majesty's subjects without distinction; and that, under these circumstances, it would be painful to his Majesty were the merit of the initiative to be snatched from him. The Congress was therefore begged not to bring forward the Polish question.

The request was acceded to; not, however, until a solemn promise had been obtained from the Russian Plenipotentiary as to certain liberal measures, and especially on the three following heads:—

A general amnesty.

The re-establishment of the Polish language.

Liberty of conscience.

The *amnesty* was, in effect, proclaimed on the 15/27 May, 1856. No longer afterwards than the month of June following, an Ukase decreed the confiscation of the property of three Poles, *for having served in the revolutionary army of Hungary* (in 1848.)

The *re-establishment of the Polish language* met with no better fate, witness the incident at Kamienec, where the Emperor Alexander refused to receive a petition on this subject, with the remark that 'he was Emperor of Russia; that he 'was on Russian soil; that those who had

'addressed him were all Russians; and that he
'would have nothing to do with Poland and the
'Poles.'*

As regards *liberty of conscience,* in order to have an idea of the manner in which it has been respected it will be sufficient to read the following document, which is dated seven years after the Congress at Paris.

Circular addressed by the military commandant of the district of Wilkomir to the Chief of the Police, Major Schlykoff.

'In consequence of the murders and robberies
'which are constantly recurring, I have resolved
'to publish in the district the following:—

'I attribute all these disorders to the *proved*
'*propensity of the Catholic clergy for brigandage and*
'*rebellion, a propensity common to the whole of that*
'*body, from the Holy Father Pius IX., and his*
'*Cardinals at Rome* down to the pastor who
'officiates in the poorest church in Lithuania. I
'therefore decree:

'1. That when brigands approach a village
'the priests shall be reminded of their duty, which

---

* *L'Eglise Catholique en Pologne,* by P. Lescœur.—Tome. I, p. 266.

'is that of going towards them with the Cross and
'the Testament, and not with bread and salt, as
'they have done hitherto. They must use per-
'suasive means, and employ all their eloquence to
'dissuade those wretches from committing crimes.
'*The rebels, finally, shall not be permitted to enter*
'*a given village without passing over the body of its*
'*priests.*

'If they do that, I shall hasten to report their
'exploits to the Bishop of Wilna and to Pope Pius
'IX. at Rome, *in order that these martyr-priests may*
'*not wait too long for their canonisation.*

'The priests who may not have obeyed these
'instructions to the letter, shall by my order be
'placed under arrest and taken before the court-
'martial, where the minutes shall be drawn up in
'twenty-four hours; and they shall be adjudged as
'having taken an active part in the insurrection.

'2. That the priests shall be held responsible
'for all the murders committed in their respective
'parishes. They shall answer *with their heads* and
'*their property* for every crime *already committed*
'or which *may yet be committed.*

'I have requested the landed gentry to co-operate in the pacification of the country by making concessions to their peasants and by adopting in their relations towards these a specially benevolent and kindly manner.

'For this reason, I have decreed:

'1. That I will immediately place the domains of such land-owners as may oppress the peasantry with unwarranted exactions under military administration. In other words, I will send garrisons *to undertake the stewardship of their estates a little.*

'I will without delay sequester the property of such land-owners as I may judge to be decidedly unfit to administer their fortunes. I will employ their revenues in pacifying the country and stamping out the rebellion.

'COLONEL MOLLER.'

'29/17 August, 1863.' (*)

We might well, perhaps, leave the reader under the impression of the disgust which cannot fail to be excited by the above document, where ferocity

---

* *Le code rouge.* Dentu, Paris, 1863, p. 36.

is mingled with a flippant cynicism. But a last duty remains to be fulfilled.

The foregoing pages contain, as we have said, a lesson. Let them likewise serve as a warning. Russia foiled in her plans at the Constantinople Conference, may try to transfer her action into another field. She may attempt once more to draw Europe into a common understanding. Now, the revelations which fill this volume cannot allow Europe to deceive herself any longer. An UNDERSTANDING with Russia henceforward can mean but one thing and be called but by one name:— COMPLICITY.

THE END.

www.ingramcontent.com/pod-product-compliance
Lightning Source LLC
Chambersburg PA
CBHW020056170426
43199CB00009B/304